FAMILY CRUCIBLE

Family Crucible

*The Influence of Family Dynamics in the
Life and Ministry of John Wesley*

Anthony J. Headley

WIPF & STOCK · Eugene, Oregon

FAMILY CRUCIBLE
The Influence of Family Dynamics in the Life and Ministry of John Wesley

Wipf & Stock
An Imprint of Wipf and Stock Publishers
199 W. 8th Ave., Suite 3
Eugene, OR 97401

www.wipfandstock.com

ISBN: 978-1-60608-001-6

Manufactured in the U.S.A.

Contents

List of Illustrations and Tables

Acknowledgements

I WISH TO THANK Asbury Theological Seminary for allowing me the sabbatical leave, which made this project possible. Through use of their faculty development funds, Asbury Theological Seminary also facilitated my travel to, and studies at, the Manchester Wesley Research Centre and Methodist Church Archives at John Rylands University Library during spring 2008. This trip gave me the unique opportunity to consult first-hand some of the original Wesley family documents.

Dr. Peter Rae, Dean of Nazarene Theological College, in conjunction with his staff, graciously helped me work out the necessary details for study at Manchester Wesley Research Centre, located at the college. I also found a gracious welcome from many persons while there, including the Administrator Dr. Herbert B. McGonigle. To all these persons, named and unnamed, I wish to express my heartfelt gratitude.

My expressions of thanks must also go to Dr. Peter Nockles of the John Rylands University Library. Dr. Nockles was very gracious in meeting with me to discuss the nature of my project and suggesting appropriate portions of the Wesley family resources which were most in keeping with my project.

Besides these, many others have played a role in bringing this project to completion. Dr. Kenneth Boyd graciously allowed me to use some of his photos of Wesley sites for this book. In addition, he arranged for me to have access to digital copies of the Wesley paintings done by Richard Douglas for inclusion in the book. When I first proposed studying John Wesley for my sabbatical project, Dr. Kenneth Collins, an acknowledged Wesley scholar, provided me with some useful resources. Similarly,

Dr. Kenneth Kinghorn suggested useful resources in my early stages of looking at John Wesley. Additionally, Ms. Cheri Cowell of Garden Gate Ministries completed the necessary editing to prepare the book for publication and approached this task with a great deal of diligence and interest. Along the way, she provided useful feedback and suggestions. Besides these persons, I have had many useful conversations with Dr. Brian Yeich, and on occasion received useful resources from him. Other members of Asbury's Information Commons including Jay Endicott, Paul Tippey, and Grace Yoder helped me with various aspects of the project such as securing permissions, using archival material, and answering varied copyright questions. I offer my heartfelt thanks to all these persons.

I also wish to thank Wipf and Stock and their representatives such as Christian Amondson for agreeing to publish this book and working with me as I sought to bring it to completion.

Finally I wish to thank my wife Adina for her encouragement as I have worked on this project. Her encouragement was more than verbal; she even read draft materials related to this project. Thank you, Adina.

Introduction

Three Influences Guiding Interest
in Wesley and his family

THE IMPACT OF FAMILY dynamics on John Wesley's life and ministry has stoked the fires of my interest and curiosity for many years. Three personal experiences ignited this interest with the first harkening back to my ministry training in Bible college and seminary. During a course on John Wesley, a classmate and I wondered about Wesley's marriage. We had heard he married and the relationship proved troublesome. Besides these broad contours of the story, we knew next to nothing about his relationship. We studied his tremendously successful work in the Methodist revival in England and his unique emphasis on Christian perfection. Given these positive discussions, we feared raising a question about this delicate area of his life would represent sounding a discordant note in an otherwise magnificent tale of heroic Christian exploits. But one day, we mustered sufficient courage to make the inquiry. From our admittedly biased perspective, the question was largely left unaddressed. We had intended no disrespect to Wesley for we merely thought the discussion might yield important lessons about life and ministry from this august figure for our own young, budding ministries. Indeed, it might have afforded us an opportunity to discuss how to resolve conjugal and ministry conflicts. Perhaps the question went unaddressed because it might have seemed an unproductive tangent, which might sully the otherwise pristine reputation of this great man of God. I can only guess at the reasons, but whatever the thinking, we never received the answers we were seeking.

Unfortunately, at times we place our heroes on pedestals and revere them too greatly. In the process, we forget they are but human. In Scripture, I have noted the different stance God takes; he is not loath to exposing the clay feet of some of his most valued servants. For example, while presenting the stellar faith of Abraham, Scripture yet presents him at some of his lowest moments: lying about Sarah being his wife (Gen 12:10–13) and his somewhat faithless taking of Hagar as his concubine (Gen 16:1–6). Even more stunningly, after presenting David as a man after his own heart, God showed the depths of his degradation in the affair with Bathsheba and his subsequent shameful ordering of her husband's death (2 Sam 11). In light of these facts, I doubt God would have a problem with discussing Wesley's marriage and its complications.

Perhaps, I partly relate this information at the outset as an apology for this book. Although I expect to discuss positive aspects of Wesley's life and ministry, I also expect to unearth some negatives, especially when discussing Wesley's intimate relationships. It is possible some reader might think me irreverent to delve into these areas of Wesley's life. To these, I say, God is willing to present both the best and the worst of his cherished servants. Besides, just as I sought answers to my questions during my ministry training without malice toward Wesley, I write today, not to do a disservice to Wesley, but to unearth truths, which, when properly examined, might prove valuable to those practicing ministry. In this sense, my purpose is primarily pastoral. Additionally, as the astute reader might guess, I seek partly to answer the question raised so many years ago, because the questions did not go way but merely went underground only to surface years later, eventuating in this project.

The second experience, which influenced the writing of this book, came from a series of lectures given several years ago at Asbury Theological Seminary. James Fowler presented the 1991 Freitas Lectures and spoke on John Wesley's pilgrimage from a developmental perspective. This was the first public presentation I had experienced, which painted a less than idyllic picture of the Epworth family. Not only did Fowler demonstrate how a developmental perspective might serve to illuminate Wesley's life, he portrayed a home characterized by some degree of enmeshment (Fowler, 1991).

The third and final experience, which brought this interest back to the foreground, occurred in August of 2003 when I had the opportunity to visit London. During this time, I made my obligatory Wesleyan pilgrimage to City Road Chapel. In the museum below, one chart presented a genealogy of the Wesley family. The genealogy reminded me of the genogram used in family therapy and ignited a renewed interest in pursuing this long dormant project, using insights drawn from the theories of Alfred Adler and Murray Bowen.

Before I begin, perhaps a caveat is in order: I do not come to this project as one trained in historical method, although I have long harbored an ardent love for history. I indulge this love of history by frequent dates with the History Channel while consulting encyclopedias to read more about the event being presented. However, beyond this love of history, which dates back to my high school days, I have no formal training in historical method. Rather, I was trained first in theology and later in psychology and family therapy methods. It is this combination of training in theology as well as in the concepts and tools of psychology and family therapy, which I bring to this project. This blend of training serves to shape my investigation and understanding of the historical Wesley's life and ministry. In this sense, the book falls into the field of Wesleyan history, but from a distinctive psychological and family-oriented perspective. By wedding historical facts with these social science concepts, I hope to bring new insights, and/or new perspectives to the life and ministry of the founder of Methodism. Despite his obvious greatness, Wesley was a lot like us: His time, culture, and family shaped the development of the person he became. These influences would shape his psychological makeup and his demonstrated approach to life and ministry. In essence, his setting and especially his family became a crucible that honed his gifts, graces, and vulnerabilities in life and ministry.

chapter 1

Two Lenses for Understanding
the Wesley Family

A Tragic Family Story

SHE REPUTEDLY POSSESSED A rare combination of brilliance and beauty. They resided side by side in stunning measure in this tall, graceful woman. For a woman of her time, she received an exceptionally good education. She possessed rare skill in writing and poetry and even published a few literary pieces in a reputable magazine. Radiant in beauty, she naturally attracted many ardent and persistent suitors for her fair hand. Alas! For his favorite and most brilliant daughter, none of these proved good enough for her father, a country parson in a rather rustic, out of the way village. He rejected one suitor after another, until the desperate daughter feared she would never find an appropriate husband. Then along came a suitor who at least matched her in brilliance. This perceived equal, who swept her off her feet, was, as is recorded in many accounts, a lawyer, though some debate this.[1] Fearing interference and another lost suitor because of her father's actions, she agreed to run away with him.

The lawyer seemed sincere. In fact, he promised marriage. The day before the proposed marriage, he lured her into bed and then callously deserted her before legally consummating the marriage, though he had done so carnally. To whom would she now turn? To compound the problem, she discovered she was pregnant, though still single—a shameful condition for any woman, especially for one of her background. She had nowhere to go. In hopeful desperation, she returned home only to face the fury of a father who felt betrayed by his favorite daughter. Forgiveness from him would not come, even though she pleaded for it. What's more,

---

1. Rack, *Reasonable Enthusiast.*

just about everyone in the family, including her mother, turned against her. She felt alone, confused, and betrayed, not only by her deceiving suitor but also by the family who ought to have forgiven and succored her during her hour of greatest need.

In order to cover the shame of this family known for their religious rectitude and its prominent standing in the community, her father did what she had deeply desired long before her elopement. He forged a relationship with a willing suitor. And what a brute of a man he chose! No education, no culture, no breeding! But at least he was a man, though some might have heatedly debated this assessment. Speedily, the irate father forced her into a marriage with this brutish fellow. Life would be hard from hereafter! And it was! Her husband, addicted to alcohol, abused her terribly through much of their marriage. What's more, some five months after her marriage to this clod, she gave birth to her treacherous lover's daughter, but the child soon died. Her grief was unbounded! And yet, she longed to finally receive her father's forgiveness and to that end, she wrote him a desperate letter, pleading for his forgiveness and reconciliation:

> Should God give and take away another (child), I can never escape the thought that my father's intercession might have prevailed against His wrath, which I shall then take to be also manifest. Forgive me, sir . . . But as you planted my matrimonial bliss so you cannot run away from my prayers when I beseech you to water it with a little kindness. My brothers will report to you what they have seen of my way of life and my daily struggle to redeem the past. But I have come to a point where I feel your forgiveness to be necessary to me. I beseech you then not to withhold it.[2]

The letter fell on deaf ears! Is there one more recalcitrant, less forgiving, and more stubbornly obstinate than a wounded, prideful father? No! He would not forgive her. And forgive her he did not. Several years after his death, her mother changed her attitude towards her daughter. By that time, most, if not all, of her siblings also reconciled with her. In fact, one of her brothers actually supported her from the very beginning of her ordeal and had chided his father publicly in sermons on universal charity and rash judgment[3]. Though pointed, his rebuke did little to promote remorse and forgiveness in the obstinate father. For the rest of her life, this brilliant

2. Maser, *Story of John Wesley's Sisters*, 62.

3. Moore, *Authority*.

and beautiful, yet humbled, daughter would bear the scars and wounds of this episode. The wounds seared more deeply and excruciatingly by the fact that her father went to his grave and never forgave her.

The broad details of this story actually happened. But the script was not borrowed from a daytime soap opera, even though it easily could have been. In fact, this is the story of Hetty Wesley, the beautiful and talented daughter of that venerable Rector of Epworth, Samuel Wesley. Moreover, the one who preached the sermon against his father's actions was his son, and the subject of this book, John Wesley. The story illustrates for us the power of family dynamics to shape human lives in powerful and sometimes even negative ways. The family forms a crucible, a God-given vessel where human lives are honed and refined, sometimes for the better and sometimes for the worse. In this repository, powerful forces converge and churn together. These forces include long-held family traditions, legacies and myths, and persistent family patterns, swirling together to shape lives placed in this cauldron. Other factors outside the internal dynamics of family life also shape individual lives. These include the confluence of macro factors within the society—economic, political, and socio-cultural—which creates powerful forces, and likewise shapes personal identity.

This shaping of individuals forms the theme of this book. Although I began with the story of Hetty, this book is not about her, but rather, it is about her famous brother, John. I have chosen to tell her story in brief as a purposeful introduction to the Wesley family and to undergird the role of family dynamics. Hetty's experience carries within it some of the implicit principles and concepts, which I will discuss in this chapter and, indeed, across the entire book. I will use her story in this chapter to briefly illustrate some of the concepts presented. In the rest of the book, these concepts will be more specifically applied to John Wesley.

As theoretical lens through which to view the Wesley family, I will primarily borrow concepts from two theorists. The first is one of my favorites, Alfred Adler. From him I will utilize the concept of the *family constellation* as well as the role of *early recollections*. I will also draw heavily from Murray Bowen and concepts discussed in his Extended Family Systems approach. Throughout this initial chapter, I will use Hetty's story to illustrate some of the concepts discussed. In so doing, I trust it will provide a basis for the reader to more easily understand the applications to the life and ministry of John Wesley.

Alfred Adler and the Formative Influence of Family

Alfred Adler was a contemporary of Sigmund Freud and, at one time, was a part of his group, the Vienna Psychoanalytic Society. Many persons have erroneously identified him as a pupil of Freud, although he was a theorist in his own right. Contrary to these opinions, Freud invited Adler to join his society after he had written two defenses of Freud's theories.[4] In my opinion, Adler serves as a more important figure for psychology and the therapeutic field than Freud because of the sheer number of approaches his theory has spawned. For example, in Adler's thought we find a precursor to cognitive approaches to therapy, especially evident in his concepts of the lifestyle and basic mistakes. The former term refers to a cognitive map which gives rise to a particular approach and direction to life. In basic mistakes, defined as errors one associates with truth, one can discern cognitive errors, which can prove troublesome. Beyond these emphases, one can also find elements, which mirror humanistic approaches. This appears in his emphasis on meaning, choice, and responsibility. Moreover, in his approach one finds embedded and implicit systems thinking about the nature of humans and their life in families. Adler himself had been greatly shaped by his family life and experiences, having grown up with rickets. One professional informed his father he was fit only to be a cobbler, but Adler defied this assessment and became a medical doctor and psychological theorist. Unfortunately, Adler does not receive enough respect. In fact, I have often termed him the Rodney Dangerfield of psychology, because he gets no respect: Many persons borrow from his embryonic thoughts without giving him credit as the source of their ideas.

Adler emphasized the role of family in the development of one's identity. We especially see this role in his concept of the *family constellation*. The family constellation involves the way in which the family is configured. It is also the system in which one develops one's sense of identity and self-concept.[5] The term is a comprehensive one which incorporates various elements of family life. It includes concepts such as birth order, family values, and atmosphere. For Adler, all behavior occurs in a social context and the family forms the primary place where such behavior takes place. In this environment one begins one's search for significance. Likewise, however, the family can contribute to individual

4. Mosak, "Adlerian Psychotherapy."

5. Corey, *Theory and Practice*, 1.

demoralization and cause one to lose a sense of significance and importance.[6] The family constellation shapes its members in other significant ways, as well. Essentially, it can shape one's direction in life—for good or ill. Moreover, family can also shape the *style of life.* The style of life or lifestyle refers to convictions, which persons develop early in life, and which helps them understand, experience, shape, and control life.[7] The family partly determines the quality of relationships one develops, and the degree of positive contributions that person offers to society. But the family environment can also complicate one's life in these areas. As a result of negative influences, it can curtail the development of healthy relationships and move one toward "the useless side of life," as Adler described it. It can contribute to a faulty approach to life, leading one to pursue faulty goals. Moreover, it can also demoralize persons, thereby creating difficulty in coping with life's challenges.[8]

However, for Adler, individuals within the family can perceive its constellation differently. Adler noted: "Curiously enough we will find that no two children, even those born in the same family, grow up in the same situation. Even within the same family, the atmosphere that surrounds each individual is quite particular."[9] Elsewhere Adler noted:

> It is a common fallacy to imagine that children of the same family are formed in the same environment. Of course there is much that is the same for all children in the same home, but the psychological situation of each child is individual and differs from that of others, because of the order of their succession. There has been some misunderstanding of my custom of classification according to the position in the family. It is not, of course, the child's number in the order of successive births which influences his character, but the *situation* into which he is born and the way in which he interprets it.[10]

In other words, the perception of the family environment differs from child to child depending upon their interpretation of their particular situation. Moreover, the interpretation partly depends upon the birth

6. Adler, *Practice and Theory.*

7. Adler, *Practice and Theory; Science of Living; Individual Psychology;* Mosak, "Adlerian Psychotherapy."

8. Adler, *Practice and Theory, Science of Living.*

9. Ibid., 44.

10. Adler, *Individual Psychology,* 376–77.

order or sibling position of the child. We find a good example of differing perceptions of one's family environment in a letter Samuel Wesley Jr. wrote to John Wesley on December 10, 1726. Samuel wrote the letter in response to the sermon titled Rash Judgment, which John preached relative to the Hetty affair. At one point in the letter, Samuel Jr. wrote, "I wish you had spared the paragraph of my father's temper. I have lived longer with him than you, and I have been very intimate, and yet almost always pleased him, and I am confident I shall do so to the end of my life. So that what you are persuaded is flatly impossible . . ."[11] Samuel Jr. obviously perceived his father's temper differently than John though both had sprung from the same household. Perhaps one can largely attribute this different perception to their age; Samuel being the eldest child, and some thirteen years older than John. In this sense, they had truly experienced different fathers. But, whether it derives from age or some other element or experience, children from the same family can possess radically different perceptions of their parents and their environments, and Samuel Junior's letter supports this reality. However, when one considers birth order, one ought not to think simply in terms of the numerical position of the child. Rather, it is the psychological position of the child and how the latter interprets their role in the family.[12] Thus, even though one might associate achievement and being the family trendsetter with eldest children, conditions in the family might allocate this role to someone else in the family. As I will demonstrate later in this book, several conditions in the Wesley family made John a signal figure and ascribed to him a primary psychological position in the family.

What elements of the Wesley family environment might one deduce from the story of Hetty Wesley told at the outset? First, in the story one discovers a patriarchal family, dominated by Samuel Wesley's rules. These rules ascribed to him the final word in choosing suitors and marriage partners for his daughters. Of course, given the dominance of males in the culture of that day, this element was not unique to the Wesleys. But, for a bright person like Hetty, this environment became stifling. One might interpret her elopement as a rebellion against harsh and confining rules. Second, in the aftermath of her pregnancy, we delineate another feature of the Wesley family betrayed in the predominant attitudes displayed towards Hetty; in relation to such matters as sexual rectitude and betrayal

11. Wesley, S. J., "Letter to John Wesley, 10 dec. 1726."
12. Adler, *Practice and Theory, Science of Living.*

of the family values, they largely mimicked the unforgiving stance and recalcitrance of their father. After all, the Rector's rule was law and few crossed him. Not even Susanna, who could be as headstrong as he, dared cross him to offer her forgiveness, love, and acceptance. Only after he died did she carve out a new relationship with Hetty.[13] Surprisingly, support for, and acceptance of, Hetty came from unexpected places. First, she received unabashed support from her crippled sister Mary. Perhaps, Mary empathized with Hetty because she also knew the sting of rejection, perceiving herself as the butt of the family's jokes.[14] Whatever her reasons, Mary threw her support solidly behind Hetty. The second source of support came from John Wesley who preached a thinly veiled sermon on rash judgment against his father's treatment of Hetty.[15]

In the concept of *family constellation*, Adler included emphases on the masculine and family guiding lines within the family. By guiding line, Adler meant the roles prescribed for males and females within a particular family. In the Wesley family, the prevailing cultural values influenced these roles. These cultural values placed priority on males and their education without corresponding emphasis on females. As a result, Samuel Wesley prioritized the formal education of his sons but not for his daughters.[16] On the other hand, the culture prescribed the role of provider for females to males in the family. Thus, the Wesley sons gave great diligence to providing for the females in their families. The eldest son Samuel demonstrated Herculean resolve in providing such care to Samuel Wesley Jr.'s death. John and Charles also helped provide for their female kin.[17]

Besides these roles dictated by cultural values, family constellation includes other roles which members play. The Wesley family correspondence makes some of these roles relatively clear. From the example given at the outset, one could likely label Hetty Wesley the "black sheep" of the family, having betrayed her family's values by becoming pregnant out of wedlock. But other roles appear such as Samuel Wesley Junior's prototypical role of the eldest child. He served as the protector and one of the chief means of financial support for the family members, including parents,

13. Maser, *Story of John Wesley's Sisters*.

14. Wesley, Mary, "Letter to John Wesley, Oxford, January 20, 1727."

15. Maser, *Story of John Wesley's Sisters*; Moore, *Authority*.

16. Clarke, *Memoirs*.

17. Edwards, *Sons to Samuel*; Wesley, S. J., "Letter to his father, 11 May 1719"; "Letter to Samuel Wesley 29 August 1719."

brothers, and sisters.[18] Emilia, the eldest girl, also played a distinctive role in the family. Her mother Susanna saw her as her trusted right hand and depended upon her for support. Sometimes family circumstances forced Emilia to curtail her own plans and independence to return home to help her mother. Emilia also played the role of caretaker, especially for her youngest sister, Kezia. Some of her correspondence reveals the emotional and financial pressure this role placed on her. In addition, Emilia played the role of the family critic, often detailing in her writings the difficulties within the family while firing her strongest barbs at her father.[19] John Wesley appeared ensconced in the central role of family star. Much of the family correspondence seemed to flow mostly to him. In fact, one catalog of the Wesley papers found at the Methodist Church Archives at the John Rylands Library held 78 family letters. Of these 78 letters, 54 were written to John, suggesting him as the central focus in his family. His sisters especially held him in high esteem and sought him out for counsel and advice about their intimate matters. In fact, of the 33 letters from them in the collection, 31 were written to John.[20]

Adlerians also speak of role models and alliances within the family constellation. Three extended family members come readily to mind when considering role models. Samuel Wesley's brother, Matthew played a significant role in the Epworth Household. However, he has received negative attention for his critique of his brother's perceived neglect of his family, particularly his daughters.[21] But he provided significant financial help and accommodation to some of the Wesley girls such as Hetty and Martha.[22] Although she has received little if any attention in the literature, which I reviewed, Anne Annesley also played an important role. Although little information about her exists, from extant family material, she appeared to have provided emotional support for her sister and was evidently engaged to some degree in the lives of her children. On her death, she bequeathed several items to Susanna's children.[23] In addition,

18. Edwards, *Sons to Samuel*.

19. Wesley, E, "Letter to John Wesley, April 7, 1725"; "Letter to John Wesley, August 13, 1735."

20. Headley, "Anne Wesley."

21. Clarke, *Memoirs*.

22. Maser, *Story of John Wesley's Sisters*.

23. Welsey, Mary, "Letter to John Wesley, January 20, 1727."

she willed a liberal inheritance to her sister and her children as detailed in the following words from Kezia Wesley written on July 3, 1734:

> Tis true my father has never been easy since we heard of my Aunt Nancy's will. She left a 1000 pounds to be paid fifty pound yearly, to my mother during her life, and then it is to be divided among her children, which has displeased my father much because he cannot dispose of it.[24]

In contrast to Anne Annesley's generosity to the Wesleys, one can raise an eyebrow over Samuel Annesley Junior's lack of charity. Initially, he appeared to have helped provide for the family, taking in his niece, Sukey, at one point. In the end, he disinherited the Epworth Wesleys, cutting them off with a shilling.[25]

Before leaving this discussion of Alfred Adler's idea of family constellation, I will raise one additional concept, which relates to unresolved issues one might carry from childhood. Here I refer to Adler's concept of early recollections and how this shapes one's direction in life.[26] Like family constellation, early recollections play a major role in shaping the identity and direction of one's life. Speaking about early recollections, Adler noted:

> When rightly understood in relation to the rest of an individual's life, his early recollections are found always to have a bearing on the central interests of that person's life. Early recollections give us hints and clues, which are most valuable when attempting the task of finding the direction of a person's striving. They are most helpful in revealing what one regards as values to be aimed for and what one senses as dangers to be avoided. They help us to see the kind of world, which a particular person feels he is living in, and the early ways he found of meeting that world. They illuminate the origins of the style of life. The basic attitudes which have guided an individual thought throughout his life and which prevail, likewise, in his present situation, and to cherish in his memory as reminders. He has preserved these as his early recollections.[27]

Hetty Wesley's escapade likely became an early family recollection. It appears the kind of story, which would burrow deeply into the psyche

24. Wesley, K., "Letter to John Wesley, July 3, 1734."
25. Maser, *Story of John Wesley's Sisters.*
26. Adler, *Practice and Theory.*
27. Adler, *Significance of Earliest Recollections*, 287.

of the whole family. It certainly shaped Hetty's life in significant ways. The event displaced her from the role of favored daughter and sent her on a futile journey of seeking her father's forgiveness. But, it also seems to have shaped her view of herself and her perception of her acceptance by others. In one letter from her later life, Hetty spoke of her uselessness to herself and others and how she wished she were good for something. Moreover, overcome by self-doubt, she feared entering one of the Methodist Bands, lest she brought shame upon her brothers.[28] Her escapade, and its aftermath, seemed to have demoralized her for the rest of her life. How unlike the young, confident woman this seems! But this family recollection even shaped John Wesley and his relationship with his father: John's sermon against his father stuck in his father's memory and might have sparked an estrangement between them.[29]

Other recollections also shaped John Wesley, and these memories truly derived from his early life. First, as we will see later, his parents' separation, prior to his birth, by his own report bore significance for his life. Indeed, Wesley took this event as the starting place for his own biography. Second, Wesley's salvation from the Epworth fire of 1709 deeply impacted him. As a result, he would, thereafter, characterize himself as "a brand plucked from the burning." The escape from the fire would shape his life and work; namely, it would set him on a lifelong pursuit of love for God, which later expressed itself in a deep commitment to ministry.

Murray Bowen and Extended Family Systems Theory

I have chosen Extended Family Systems theory formulated by Murray Bowen as the second lens for viewing John Wesley. Bowen placed differentiation of the self at the heart of his model.[30] Speaking about differentiation of the self, Bowen wrote: "The one most central theoretical premise of family systems theory concerns the degree to which we all have poorly "differentiated" selfs (sic), or the degree to which we are "undifferentiated," or the degree of our unresolved emotional attachments to families of origin."[31] Speaking to the centrality of this concept, Nichols noted: ". . . unresolved emotional attachment to one's family must be resolved rather

---

28. Wright, "Letter from Bristol, July 13, 1744."
29. Moore, *Authority*.
30. Bowen, *Family Therapy*.
31. Bowen, *Family Therapy*, 529.

than passively accepted or reactively rejected, before one can differentiate into a mature, healthy personality."[32] For Bowen, differentiation of the self is necessary in order to a form a healthy self.

One can think of differentiation in both intrapsychic and interpersonal terms. Intrapsychic differentiation highlights the need to distinguish between one's thinking and one's feelings rather than confuse the two. Undifferentiated persons confuse the two constantly. This form of differentiation permits one to maintain their own sense of self, even when involved in intense emotional relationships.[33] On the other hand, interpersonal differentiation points to the need to distinguish oneself from others.[34] This capacity permits one to experience intimacy in relationships while maintaining a sense of personal autonomy. Differentiation also allows an individual to remain in a tension and disagreement-filled relationship without emotionally distancing just to preserve one's sense of self.[35] For Bowen, differentiation of the self-expresses itself through a variety of interlocking concepts. These include the following: 1. nuclear family emotional process, 2. the family emotional process, 3. multigenerational transmission process, 4. sibling position and, 5. emotional triangles. I will briefly describe each of these concepts below to provide a basis for understanding their application to the life and ministry of John Wesley.

Nuclear Family Emotional Process

By this term, Bowen referred to the emotional forces operating in families in recurrent patterns. Because they lack differentiation, families tend to emotionally fuse to each other. Although this may serve as the family's normal way of operating, sometimes the closeness becomes too stifling and members react to it by distancing from each other. Families might distance through internal mechanisms such as emotional distancing or even through physical illness or depression. Or they might do it by physically distancing from the family.[36] Bowen used the term *cut-off* to describe these forms of distancing.[37]

32. Nichols, *Family Therapy*, 349.

33. Bowen, *Family Therapy*; Nichols, *Family Therapy*; Nichols and Schwartz, *Family Therapy*.

34. Ibid.

35. Skowron, "Differentiation of Self."

36. Blessing, "Murray Bowen's"; Skowron, "Differentiation of Self."

37. Bowen, *Family Therapy*.

As we will see later in this book, the Wesley family exhibited a heightened degree of closeness, which fits Bowen's idea of fusion. As a result, they intimately involved themselves in each other's lives. Although this contributed to their demonstrated care for each other, especially in financial matters, some negative outcomes derived from it. For example, they interfered with each other's lives, often causing relationship difficulties and complications.[38] We can possibly perceive Hetty's elopement both as a result of this closeness and as a rebellion against it. Her elopement with her lover constituted both emotional and physical distancing from her family, but her father's and the family's refusal to forgive her, and their subsequent alienation from her, also involved emotional and physical distancing.

Family Projection Process

Bowen used this concept to describe the immaturity and tendency to fusion, which parents can project onto their offspring. Much of the time, the offspring is the one who is closest to the parent.[39] As I will demonstrate later, Samuel and Susanna seemed to have projected this tendency to fusion to all of their offspring.

Multigenerational Transmission Process

This concept refers to the replication of family patterns across succeeding generations. McGoldrick and Gerson expressed the nature of this concept well when they noted: "Families repeat themselves. What happens in one generation will often repeat itself in the next, i.e. the same issues tend to be played out from generation to generation, though the actual behavior may take a variety of forms."[40] As we will see, several patterns in the Wesley family fit this definition. On the positive side, one can point to patterns such as faith commitments, love of education and learning, and creative talents for writing and poetry. On the negative side, the family continued to experience difficult marriages across the generations usually eventuating in some form of cut-off. Hetty's difficult marriage serves as but one unfortunate example of both traits evident in Wesley family conjugal relationships. Similar difficulties characterized John Wesley's

---

38. Curnock, "The Journal of the Rev. John"; Maser, *Story of John Wesley's Sisters*.

39. Nichols, *Family Therapy*; Nichols and Schwartz, *Family Therapy*.

40. McGoldrick and Gerson, *Genograms in Family Assessment*, 5.

marriage. Another unfortunate pattern involved problems with finances across the generations, which will be discussed in more detail later.

Sibling Position

This concept reminds one of Adler's idea of birth order. According to Bowen, persons tend to develop certain fixed characteristics based on their position in the family. As noted earlier in our discussion of Adler, one should not think about this in rigid ways. It does allow for some flexibility. To this author, it would include Adler's idea of psychological position. As indicated earlier, Samuel Wesley Junior played the typical role of the eldest child. He seemed a protector who looked out for his entire family, especially in financial matters. The eldest girl, Emilia seemed more as an emotional barometer of the family's life. As I will suggest in a later chapter, the circumstances of his birth and his position in the family, likely made John Wesley the family star.

Emotional Triangles

For Bowen, a two-person relationship tends to exhibit instability because of its difficulty handling anxiety and other emotional tensions in the dyad. Outside forces can also disturb the dyad. When anxiety increases, making the dyadic relationship uncomfortable, the couple inevitably will involve a third person (or thing) to diffuse the anxiety.[41] The Hetty incident demonstrated some triangulation: John's preaching of the sermon on rash judgment can be interpreted as his triangulation in the anxious relationship between his father and Hetty. Moreover, rather than speak directly to his father about his disagreement with him relative to Hetty, John chose to make it the subject of a sermon. By this action, he triangulated his hearers into the family affair. His father's response betrayed the same tendency: rather than speak directly to John, Samuel laid his complaints about the sermon to Charles. Later, others such as Samuel Jr. also got triangulated, choosing to chide John about his sermon against his father.[42]

41. Bowen, *Family Therapy.*
42. Wesley, "Letter to John Wesley, 10 dec. 1726."

The Genogram in Extended Family Systems Theory

The family genogram serves as a tool designed to depict these varied concepts. It constitutes a family map, which captures the structure and relationships within a family. McGoldrick and Gerson define it as "a format for drawing a family tree that records information about family members and their relationships over at least three generations. Genograms display family information graphically in a way that provides a quick gestalt of complex family patterns and a rich source of hypotheses about how a clinical problem may be connected to the family context and the evolution of both problem and context over time."[43] Genograms look like a family tree. They utilize their own distinctive symbols for generating the graphic picture of the family. Based on data from eminent Wesley historian, Frank Baker,[44] I have generated a simple genogram of the Wesley family in figure 1 below. I say 'simple,' because I do not try to capture other generations in the family tree. I have also not attempted to capture all the historical and relationship information. I merely present the Samuel and Susanna and their known children, both living and dead, together with their respective birth dates.

Perusal of this genogram provides some initial orientation to the format. For example, it presents children in chronological order from left to right. In marital relationships, males are generally placed on the left and females on the right. The rectangles and circles with the "X" indicate persons who died. A square represents males, whereas circles represent females. In some cases, two-persons such as Annesley and Jedidiah are joined by two lines, forming the shape of a triangle. This denotes them as twins. Finally, the genogram contains a double line to represent John Wesley. This denotes him the focal point of our discussion. The X along the couple line between Samuel and Susanna indicate a separation occurred between them. Besides listing persons in a family, one can also list other sorts of data. For example, one can provide historical dates, including the birth and death of persons in the family. One can also utilize symbols, which indicate the nature of relationships within the family including examples of cutoff and enmeshment. By tracking these relationship patterns, one can discover the strengths and vulnerabilities of the family as

---

43. McGoldrick and Gerson, *Genograms in Family Assessment*, 1.

44. Baker, "Investigating."

FIGURE 1.1 The Wesley Nuclear Family[45]

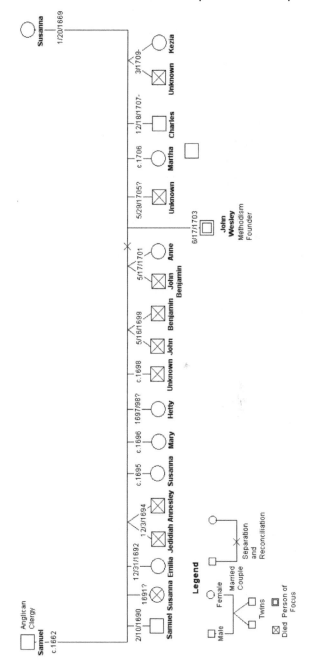

45. Based on data from Frank Baker, "Investigating."

well as highlight significant life cycle events within a family.[46] Beyond its use in clinical practice for assessing family functioning and relationships, the genogram can serve other purposes. McGoldrick and colleagues noted its usage by family physicians to record family medical history and even to chart the field of family practice and family medicine.[47] They also highlighted its value in charting the lives of historical figures and other famous persons.[48]

The genogram allows one to largely capture difficulties at a number of systems levels; namely, it permits one to capture and pay attention to the entire ecosystem. The ecosystem includes the individual, the immediate family, the extended family, the community in which they are embedded, and the larger society. Within the larger society, one must consider sociocultural, political, and economic events and how these impinge on the family.[49] Moreover, these authors have utilized the concepts of vertical and horizontal stressors to explain stress and difficulties within families, which can be captured in the genogram. By vertical stressors, the authors refer to patterns, which have been handed down to the family. At a macro level, these include factors such as sexism, classism, and poverty. At the family level, vertical stressors include generational patterns such as myths, secrets, and legacies, which influence their functioning. On the other hand, horizontal stressors refer to the anxiety generated as families move across time, trying to cope with developmental (normative) and non-normative events. The former involves normal life cycle transitions such as births and deaths; the latter includes unpredictable events such as untimely deaths and chronic illnesses. One can also consider historical events such as natural disasters, the prevailing political climate, war, and economic depression.[50]

Several of these concepts can help us understand the Wesley family. The emphasis on systems levels suggests we must pay attention not only to personal factors but also to the nuclear family, extended family, and larger societal factors. Thus, we will best understand John Wesley's life and ministry by paying attention to these other systems. Besides

46. McGoldrick and Gerson, et al., *Genograms: Assessment and Intervention.*

47. Ibid.

48. McGoldrick and Gerson, *Genograms in Family Assessment.*

49. McGoldrick and Gerson, et al., *Genograms.*

50. McGoldrick and Gerson, *Genograms in Family Assessment.*

paying attention to nuclear family dynamics, one might also consider the contributions of extended family players such as Matthew Wesley, Anne Annesley, and Samuel Annesley Junior to the family's functioning. Moreover, one should consider the impact of sociocultural, political, and economic events, which characterized British society of his day. Although I will not discuss these events to a large extent, I will briefly raise some of the broader social factors, which impinged on the Wesleys. Besides these, one ought to consider various generational patterns such as poverty and relationship difficulties. On the positive side, traditions such as religious faith, education, and learning exerted constructive influence on the family. I will discuss several of these factors in ensuing chapters. Moreover, when one considers horizontal stressors, one discovers several events, mostly of the unpredictable sort, which exerted pressure on the family. These included problems such as debt, chronic illness, several untimely deaths, and two devastating fires. All of these events significantly impacted the family and its members and doubtlessly exerted considerable influence on John Wesley's life and ministry.

Current Use of Bowen's Theory

Besides the usages suggested above, many have used Bowen's theory in the family therapy field. It has become a staple in marital and family therapy practices for understanding how families relate, function, and develop symptoms. Additionally, it has served to provide therapeutic guidance in the helping process. Moreover, some have used the approach to understand life within religious organizations. We see this approach in Edwin Friedman's classic book, *From Generation to Generation: Family Process in Church and Synagogue*. Friedman used Bowen's system concepts to describe relationships within congregational life.[51] Following Friedman's lead, Peter Steinke used the same approach to speak about emotional processes within congregational life in two of his books: *How Your Church Family Works: Understanding Congregations as Emotional Systems*[52] and *Healthy Congregations*.[53] Some writers have utilized the theory for other purposes within Christian circles. For example, Kamila Blessing[54] used

51. Friedman, *From Generation to Generation*.
52. Steinke, *How Your Church Family Works*.
53. Steinke, *Healthy Congregations*.
54. Blessing, "Murray Bowen's."

the theory as a hermeneutical tool for interpretation of the story of the prodigal son. In another work, Blessing argued for the application of Bowen's theory in interpreting the whole of the biblical text since families drive much of its content. She provided relevant examples from the gospel of John, Galatians, and Romans.[55] Given this reality, Blessing argued for the use of systems models such as Bowen's to provide insights into the many family situations evident in biblical narratives.[56] In line with such thinking, she noted an increased interest in using psychological theories in biblical interpretation.[57] I agree with Blessing's conclusion. In keeping with this conviction, even prior to reading Blessing's work, I used Bowen's model to understand and highlight dynamics within the family of Abraham, Isaac, and Jacob as described in the book of Genesis. Given the application of this model to biblical figures and their families who lived long ago, it seems to make sense to use this approach with figures of more recent vintage. Additionally, as we have already seen, McGoldrick and colleagues have used this approach to investigate historical figures.[58] I now seek to apply this approach to John Wesley and his family. This endeavor is aided by the great deal of extant material on the Wesleys, and John in particular; reputedly, more autobiographical data on John Wesley exists than on any other leader in Christian history.[59]

55. Blessing, *Psychology and the Bible.*

56. Blessing, "Murray Bowen's"; *Psychology and the Bible.*

57. Blessing, "Murray Bowen's."

58. McGoldrick and Gerson, *Genograms in Family Assessment*; McGoldrick and Gerson, et al., *Genograms.*

59. Moore, *Authority.*

chapter 2

The World of the Wesleys

A S IT IS WITH all of us, the historical period and the prevailing culture shaped the Wesleys. For example, economic factors, especially poverty and debt, significantly impacted the family. In the previous chapter, I described these factors as representing vertical stressors; that is, patterns handed down through the family. At the macro level, they include factors such as classism and poverty. But vertical stressors can also operate at the family level and include ancestral myths, secrets, and legacies.[1] Doubtless, both types of vertical stressors significantly affected the Wesley family, including the subject of our study, John Wesley. We can also use the term *ecosystem* as a corresponding term, which helps us understand the world of the Wesleys. Among these multiple systems, one can think about the individual, nuclear family, the extended family, and the larger communal systems. The latter system includes the societal factors mentioned earlier: the sociocultural, political, and economic.[2]

Whether one speaks about vertical stressors or the ecosystem, these factors significantly impacted the Wesley family. The influence of these elements on the Wesley family constitutes the focus of this chapter. I will discuss this at two levels. First, I will consider the impact of macro vertical stressors or larger ecosystem pressures on the Wesley family. Here, although other issues could be raised, I will briefly discuss two major factors. First, I will discuss the political climate, especially as it relates to problems and disputes over kingship. As we will see later, one such dispute ostensibly contributed to a rift between Samuel and Susanna Wesley. Second, I will briefly discuss the Act of Uniformity because of its implications for persecution of the dissenting ancestors of the Wesleys.

1. McGoldrick and Gerson, *Genograms in Family Assessment*; McGoldrick, et al., *Genograms*.

2. Ibid.

However, in comparison to the discussion of factors within the Wesley family, I will treat these larger societal factors relatively briefly. Several reasons dictate this imbalance. First, as a psychologist dealing with historical data, I am acutely aware of my inability to do justice to these historical events. Second, I am sure the reader can find and consult more extensive treatment of these issues. Third, from a practical standpoint, although important, these macro systems do not constitute a key focus of this book. Rather, my primary purpose is to try to understand Wesley through his immediate and extended family context. However, given the importance of the macro factors, some brief background is important for our discussion.

Macro Factors Which Shaped the Wesley Family

Disputes over Monarchs

Several factors within the society of the day clearly impinged on the Wesley family. The most visible point of influence appeared in a rift, which developed between Samuel and Susanna in 1701 over the rightful king. The dispute centered on William of Orange's claim to the English throne.[3] William of Orange came to the English throne in 1689 in the so-called "glorious revolution" when the English parliament asked him to become king in the place of James 11. James 11 had ascended the throne in 1685 on the death of his brother Charles 11. However, James incurred the wrath of the English people for several reasons. He had converted to Roman Catholicism and wanted to reclaim England to this faith. Besides this, James ran afoul of parliament in his efforts to grasp greater power for himself. Given these factors and others, some in England desired a different king. They found a willing volunteer in William of Orange who had married James 11's daughter Mary. Because of the family linkage, Mary could make legitimate claim to the throne and William used this to insist on being made king. Besides this, William and Mary ascribed themselves to the protestant faith, making them more appealing to the English than the Catholic James 11. Having laid claim to the throne, William invaded England in 1688. But before any battle could ensue, James' army deserted and he fled to France. Thus, William came to the throne in somewhat dubious circumstances, including the rather odd, but all too common

---

3. Clarke, *Memoirs.*

mixture of religion and politics.[4] Because of these events, some such as Susanna could rightly question the legitimacy of his claim to the throne.

But long before this time, the mixture of politics and religions had come together to create tensions within the realm leading up to William of Orange's ascension to the throne. Under the reign of Elizabeth 1 from 1558, England had experienced a long period of relative peace and stability, although new scholarship has criticized her latter years.[5] However, her death in 1603 brought new challenges to the kingdom. Because she died without children, she named James VI of Scotland her heir and he became James 1 of England. James 1 achieved some success in keeping his country from the turbulence, which enveloped France and other parts of Europe. He also kept his country out of The 30 Years War (1618–1648), which waged on the continent.[6] However, James also experienced problems. Because he was a Scotsman, the English disliked him. More, importantly, whereas Elizabeth and the other Tudor monarchs had worked relatively closely with parliament, James and his successors failed to maintain this close working relationship. In turn, parliament became critical of him and his policies. The House of Commons, having gained power during the reign of the Tudor monarchs, constantly differed with the Stuarts over money, thinking them gross spendthrifts. Moreover, some thought their policies had contributed to increase in prices in the general populace and resulting economic hardships.[7]

Besides the tensions over power and money, these parties also disagreed over religion. Charles 1, the successor to James 1, clashed with the Puritans over religion because of his desire for episcopal leadership in the church. Such promotion would have given Charles more power in religious issues since he appointed these leaders. Through his Archbishop William Laud, Charles pursued more elaborate rituals within the church. On the other side, the Puritans and other groups preferred more simple worship.[8] One reason for this preference was ostensibly because more elaborate rituals raised again the specter of Roman Catholicism. These groups also desired more involvement of the people in making church law. The House of Commons aligned themselves more closely with the latter perspectives on

4. Black, New History of England; Grolier, "New Book of Knowledge."
5. Ibid.
6. Black, New History of England.
7. Black, New History of England; Grolier, "New Book of Knowledge."
8. Grolier, "New Book of Knowledge."

religion. Subsequently, they sought to bend Charles to their will and desire by using the power they held over granting money to the king. To circumvent their power over money, Charles increased customs and demanded forced loans. He even took a more extreme route, choosing to rule without parliament for 11 years (1629–1640) while levying taxes.[9]

Ironically, Charles' own actions contributed to his recall of parliament in 1640. He angered the Scots when he tried to impose on them a version of the English Book of Common Prayer. In response, the Scottish invaded England. This event forced Charles to recall parliament to appropriate the money needed for war. But once in session, the members of parliament chose not to disband. They met for 13 years. This parliament was appropriately called the long parliament. Because of the continued clashes over money and religion among other issues, two civil wars developed during Charles' reign.[10] The first civil war took place between 1642 and 1645, ending with Charles' defeat. He was pressured to accept a constitutional monarchy, but instead remained defiant and tried to enlist Scotland in his fight with England. These events led to a second civil war from 1648–1649 and ended with Charles' trial and beheading and the establishment of an English republic under Oliver Cromwell.[11]

After Oliver Cromwell died, his son, Richard, proved incapable of leading England and the English reverted to a monarchy in 1660 with the ascension of Charles 1's son to the throne as Charles 11.[12] When Charles 11 died in 1685 without a legitimate child to ascend the throne, his brother James 11 became king. As indicated earlier, the latter's Roman Catholicism and desire to reconvert England brought William of Orange into the picture. The now disputed issue of rightful kingship would become the source of tension between Samuel and Susanna. Susanna apparently held to Jacobean tendencies seeing James 11 as the rightful king, whereas Samuel fully accepted William of Orange as king. The ostensible reason for the dispute would end with William's death in 1702. Since William and Mary had no children to succeed them, Mary's sister Anne became queen from 1702–1714. Apparently, both Samuel and Susanna could support her legitimate claim to the throne, ending their dispute.[13]

9. Ibid.
10. Grolier, "New Book of Knowledge."
11. Black, New History of England; Grolier, "New Book of Knowledge."
12. Grolier, "New Book of Knowledge."
13. Clarke, Memoirs.

The Act of Uniformity

All during these years, differences in religion ran hand in hand with tensions over power and money. Broadly speaking, the clash over religion largely existed between two groups. One the one hand, there were those who espoused episcopal leadership and absolute monarchy. On the other hand, there were Presbyterians who favored a church government, which included presbyters or some combination of presbyters and bishops, and a limited monarchy.[14] After much wrangling over several years, parliament eventually passed the Act of Uniformity in 1662 during the reign of Charles 11. This act represented a resounding victory for episcopal leadership. It mandated the use of the Book of Common Prayer in all Church of England services. It also demanded ordination by episcopal leaders as well as conformity to the beliefs and practices of the Church of England.[15] Those who failed to ascribe to its mandates suffered persecution and ejection from their parishes, as well as the loss of positions in universities. By 1662, some 2029 clergy including lecturers and fellows found themselves ejected from various positions.[16] Later, the act would exclude any dissenters from holding office and those of the Catholic faith found themselves excluded both from holding office and serving in parliament.[17]

This act bears significance for the Wesleys because their ancestors found themselves on the wrong side of this religious controversy and public policy. As a result, they suffered ejection from their places of ministry. In the process, some experienced significant hardships. Samuel Annesley, the father of Susanna found himself among this group who were persecuted. In fact, he served as a signer to a memorial presented to Charles 11 protesting various issues proceeding from the Act of Uniformity. He, too, would suffer ejection from his parish at St. Giles, Cripplegate in 1662 for violation of the said act.[18] However, although the Act prevented the ordination of ministers except by the established church, Samuel ordained presbyters in defiance of the ejection. He eventually became pastor of a dissenting congregation on Bishopsgate Street and there prospered. However, he did not totally escape persecution. In 1681, the government

---

14. Ibid.

15. Clarke, *Memoirs*; Dallimore, *Susanna*; Watts, *Dissenters*.

16. Watts, *Dissenters*.

17. Clarke, *Memoirs*; Dallimore, *Susanna*; Watts, *Dissenters*.

18. Clarke, *Memoirs*; Rogal, *Susanna Annesley Wesley*.

fined Samuel Annesley and several of his colleagues some 9,680 English pounds for preaching illegally.[19]

Other Wesley progenitors suffered far more greatly than Samuel Annesley. Bartholomew Wesley, the great grandfather of John Wesley was deprived of his parish at Charmouth in 1662. Thereafter, he provided for himself and his family by following the trade of an apothecary. John Wesley, Bartholomew's son and the grandfather of John Wesley experienced even greater suffering. Like many others, he suffered ejection from his parish. At the time of his ejection he served at Winterborn/ Whitchurch in Dorsetshire.[20] This ejection took place some four months before Samuel Wesley, John's father, was born. Following the ejection, John Wesley the elder apparently moved from town to town preaching in violation of the Act of Uniformity. As a result, the authorities arrested him on several occasions.[21] John Wesley, the elder, eventually fell ill and died at the relatively young age of 42, leaving his wife and small children, including Samuel Wesley, in dire poverty.[22] These early circumstances likely contributed to the trail of poverty, which would bedevil Samuel Wesley and his Epworth household for some time.

Micro Factors

The Power of Multigenerational Transmission Process

Besides stressors issuing from the larger society, pressures within the family also impacted them. Largely, these revolved around traditions and generational patterns passed down through the Wesley and Annesley families. Some of these patterns readily appear when one considers the family genogram indicated below.

A Vibrant Christian Tradition

Several conclusions emerge from the genogram. First, clergy formed a prominent part of the family tradition on both sides of the family. Both Samuel and Susanna proceeded from a long line of clergy. Additionally,

---

19. Rogal, *Susanna Annesley Wesley*.
20. Clarke, *Memoirs*; Rogal, *Susanna Annesley Wesley*.
21. Rogal, *Susanna Annesley Wesley*.
22. Clarke, *Memoirs*; Dallimore, *Susanna*; Rogal, *Susanna Annesley Wesley*.

FIGURE 2.1 A Four Generational Genogram of
the Wesley and Annesley Families[23]

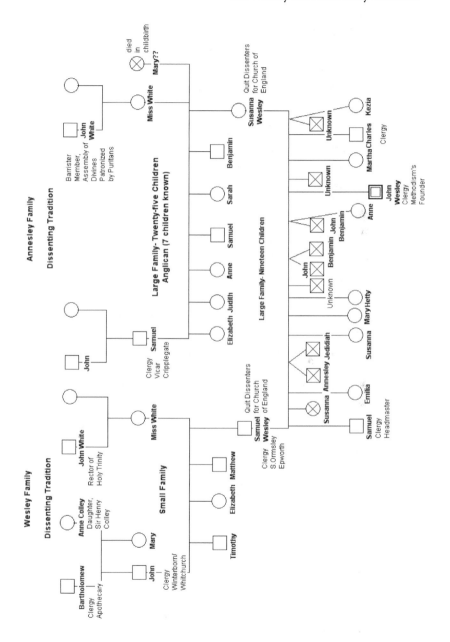

23. The information in this genogram comes from the amalgamation of a number of
sources, including Clarke, *Memoirs*; Rogal, *Susanna Annesley Wesley*.

both were reared in dissenting traditions. Dating back to Bartholomew, the Wesleys suffered greatly for embracing and maintaining this tradition. Notwithstanding this background, Samuel and Susanna came to embrace the Church of England through independent reasoning processes.[24] Samuel arrived at his decision after a course of reading designed to counter invectives against the dissenters. Instead, his reading led him to renounce his dissenting church tradition and embrace the Church of England.[25] Speaking about this, Clarke remarked:

> He lived at that time with his mother and an old aunt, both of whom were too strongly attached to the dissenting doctrines to have borne any patience to the disclosure of his design. He, therefore, got up one morning at a very early hour, and, without acquainting any one with his purpose, set out on foot to Oxford, and entered himself of Exeter College.[26]

But just as he intended to vigorously defend the Dissenters, he now turned his energies to defending the Church of England against the same Dissenters. He apparently approached this task with zeal, which outstripped concern for Christian moderation. Not surprisingly, this action placed him at odds with the Dissenters and contributed to ongoing calamity for him and his family.[27] His critique of the dissenting movement even became a source of contention within his extended family. It clearly impacted his relationship with his brother-in-law, John Dunton. Speaking about Samuel Wesley, Dunton recorded:

> I shall add my old Friend Mr. *Samuel Wesley* to the list of these Conformists. He was educated upon charity in a private Academy, if we may take his own word for it in his late Pamphlet, which was designedly written to expose and overthrow those Academies. One would have thought that either gratitude, or his own reputation in the world, and among his Relations and his best Friends, might have kept him silent, though, when a man is resolved to do himself a mischief, who can help it. But it is certainly so—*Apostata est osor sui ordinis.*[28]

24. Clarke, *Memoirs*; Dobree, *Biography of John Wesley.*

25. Clarke, *Memoirs.*

26. Clarke, *Memoirs*, 89.

27. Clarke, *Memoirs.*

28. Dunton, *Life and Errors*, 163–64.

Like her husband Samuel, Susanna reasoned her way out of the Dissenting tradition into the fold of the Church of England. Again, Clarke provided some insight into this transition:

> Under the parental roof, and before she was thirteen years of age, she examined without restraint the whole controversy between the Established Church and the Dissenters. The issue of which was, she renounced her religious fellowship with the latter, and adopted the creed and forms of the Church of England; to which she faithfully and zealously adhered as long as she lived.[29]

Susanna provided her own account of her transition from the dissenters to the Church of England:

> And because I had been educated among the Dissenters, and there being something remarkable in my leaving them at so early an age, not being full thirteen, I had drawn up an account of the whole transaction, under which I included the main of the controversy between them and the Established Church, as far as it had come to my knowledge.[30]

Given her tender age, one would think, her father would have objected to such a move. But he evidently did not object to this change in her faith or her later marriage, at a later date to a Church of England clergyman.[31] However, although her father did not hinder her move, some authors think the change strained the relationship between them.[32]

Given the strong religious background in both families, Samuel and Susanna brought a Christian heritage and a rich theological tradition into their nuclear families. Given Samuel's theological training, one would expect this of him. However, quite surprisingly, when one peruses the extant material on the Wesley family, one discovers a theological astuteness in Susanna. Various letters written to her son John supports this conclusion. He often sought her opinion on various theological matters and she responded with knowledgeable insight. I offer examples from three letters to John, which support her theological reasoning. First, we see this ability demonstrated in one letter written to John in February of 1732. In the

29. Clarke, *Memoirs*, 319.

30. Kirk, *Mother of The Wesleys*, 57.

31. Clarke, *Memoir*.

32. Dallimore, *Susanna*.

letter, she discussed issues such as the presence of Christ in the communion. She also provided a comment on the nature of the Lord's affliction:

> He had no irregular passions or sinful appetites ever to combat with, but he had what may, infinitely harder to be sustained, the greatest contradiction of sinners against the purity of his nature.[33]

Susanna Wesley based on a painting from the Epworth Old Rectory. A painting by Richard Douglas at Asbury Theological Seminary. Used with Permission.

In a similar vein, her theological ability shone through in a letter to John on a biblical discussion of temptation. In that letter, Susanna shared her opinions regarding the participation of sincere Christians in activities such as masquerades, balls, and similar pastimes. Although she did not declare these activities totally off limits for a Christian, she declared she had not known such a thing in her lifetime.[34] Again, in another letter written to John on January 1, 1734, Susanna agreed with John on the different degrees of virtues and piety and his opinion regarding William Law.[35] One of the most astounding examples of her ability appeared in a long treatise she wrote to her daughter Susanna, when the latter lived with Uncle Matthew Wesley, following the Epworth fire of 1709. This letter seems remarkable for her detailed explication of the chief articles of

33. Welsey, Susanna, "Letter to John Wesley, 21 Feb. 1732."
34. Wesley, Susanna, "Photographic copy of a letter," 25 Oct, 1732."
35. Welsey, Susanna, "Letter to John Wesley," Jan 1 1734."

the faith, primarily those based on the Apostles' Creed. In fact, Susanna expounded on the Apostles' Creed, phrase by phrase, for some twenty pages of the twenty-seven-page treatise. For example, Susanna provided the following commentary on the phrase "I believe In God:"

> I do truly and heartily assent to the being of a God, one supreme, independent Power, who is a Spirit infinitely wise, holy, good, just, true, unchangeable.
>
> I do believe that this God is a necessary, self-existent Being; necessary, in that he could not but be, because he derives his existence from no other than himself; but he always is.[36]

Perhaps her demonstrated ability in ecclesial matters drew the great crowds to the meetings she held during her husband's absence at the end of 1711 or the beginning of 1712. During his absence, Susanna conducted services for her children. Later, her neighbors requested her to allow them to attend. Her meetings drew crowds of 200 to 300. Inman, the curate whom Samuel had left in charge of the parish, became quite upset about these matters and wrote to Samuel Wesley to complain. Subsequently, Samuel wrote her, asking her to desist but she would not. Her response to Samuel indicated the popularity of her meetings: whereas before, 20–25 would attend evening service, she now drew crowds of 200–300.[37]

As one would expect, Samuel also significantly influenced his family, especially his sons. In *Sons to Samuel*, Edwards[38] discussed four key areas in which Samuel influenced his sons: 1. Love of books and learning; 2. A sturdy orthodoxy with a strong evangelical emphasis; 3. Love of the Anglican Church, its liturgy and sacraments; and 4. A vision of a world-wide-church and missionary zeal. Using the language of Bowen's theory, Samuel's influence constitutes an example of multigenerational transmission process. Some comment on these values is in order. First, as some readers might be aware, Samuel wrote hymns and poetry, as did his sons. Significantly, his influence in this area extended to at least one of his daughters, the brilliant Hetty Wesley. Samuel was also a biblical scholar familiar with the Greek and Hebrew texts and apparently a competent interpreter of Scripture. This trait evidently influenced John's writing and work and likely contributed to the strong Scriptural tenor in

36. Clarke, *Memoirs*, 354–55.
37. Ibid.
38. Edwards, *Sons to Samuel*.

Charles Wesley's hymns.[39] Second, Samuel influenced his sons in their strong commitment to orthodoxy and an equally strong emphasis on evangelical themes. Third, they imbibed from him a love of the Anglican Church, including their love of the sacraments and liturgy. Perhaps it was this transmitted love of the Anglican Church, which kept Wesley in it while at the same time sowing the seeds of Methodism's separation from her mother church. For this reason, Edwards described Wesley as an ecclesiastical schizophrenic.[40] The term seems rather strong but it conveys John Wesley's strong generational allegiance to the Anglican Church even while he moved away from it in some of his practices.

Finally, Samuel shared with his sons, especially John and Charles, his vision of the church as a worldwide body, and missionary interests in its activity.[41] Long before John and Charles left for America, Samuel embraced his own missionary plans and ambitions. In his thirties, he planned to go as a missionary to China, India, or Abyssinia. Furthermore, he proposed a plan for missions in a paper to Archbishop Sharp, although his proposal was not adopted.[42] Samuel also developed interest in Oglethorpe's Georgia colony and wrote the following words to him in 1734:

> I had always so dear a love of your colony that if it had been but ten years ago, I would gladly have devoted the remainder of my life and labours to that place and think I might before this time have conquered the language without which little can be done among the natives.[43]

Because he could not go, at that time he tried to persuade Oglethorpe to take John Whitelamb, his assistant and husband to Mary Wesley.[44] Clearly, Samuel harbored unfulfilled missionary dreams. Significantly, six months after his father's death, John boarded the Simmonds for his sojourn in Georgia. Two days before, having completed the writing of his father's dissertation on the book of Job, John presented it to Queen Caroline to whom Samuel had dedicated it.[45] The presentation to the

39. Ibid.
40. Ibid.
41. Ibid.
42. Clarke, *Memoirs*.
43. Edwards, *Family Circle*, 29.
44. Ibid.
45. Clarke, *Memoirs*.

queen served to fulfill his father's dream. Perhaps the trip to America also served to fulfill another unrequited dream of his father's.

The Clash of Family Cultures

Although the marriage between Samuel Wesley and Susanna Annesley combined a rich religious heritage, it also brought challenges with which they would need to wrestle. Based on observations from their family genogram presented earlier, I now draw attention to several possible challenging issues. These challenges would arise from the clash of their different family cultures. First, one notes the tradition of extremely large families on the Annesley side. Samuel Annesley, Susanna's father, reputedly fathered some twenty-five children, with Susanna being the youngest. But Samuel Annesley possessed much greater financial resources to support such a sizable family.[46] In contrast, the Wesley side comprised smaller families in the previous generations. This differing tradition of family size might have had some impact on Susanna and Samuel's marriage. Could Samuel's experience with smaller families have caused him to balk at the rapidly growing size of his family, especially given his debts and earnings? One wonders about this, especially when one considers the kind of comments Samuel made about his growing family. Some of the comments appear almost callous. On May 18, 1701, Samuel wrote to Archbishop John Sharpe and commented about the birth of a boy and a girl. This evidently referred to the birth of the twins, Anne and John Benjamin, who were the twelfth and thirteenth child born to them. In the same letter, Samuel commented on having had had four children born in two years and a day.[47] The other two were the twin boys John and Benjamin who would later die. In another letter, Samuel spoke about his wife lying about sick and having children and many servants to provide for.[48] These comments suggest possible frustration in Samuel, most likely due to the financial pressures his growing family brought. Perhaps, these comments also arose from being unaccustomed to having so many children, having come from a much smaller family and the inability to adequately care for them. One even wonders if this proposed discomfort contributed to his desertion of Susanna and the growing brood of children. Of course, one

46. Dallimore, *Susanna*.
47. Welsey, Samuel, "Letter to Archbishop," May 18, 1701.
48. Dallimore, *Susanna*.

cannot say this definitively, but based on the pattern in the genogram, it seems plausible.

The family data gleaned during the construction of the genogram reveals another stark contrast in the Annesley and Wesley families. The Annesleys possessed greater financial resources than the Wesley family. Samuel Annesley, Susanna's father apparently did not suffer financial adversity from the Act of Uniformity and the forced resignation of his pastorate at Cripplegate. His family continued to do well financially. At his death, he left a sizable fortune to three of his children.[49] The story appears patently different on the Wesley side of the family. The Wesleys experienced impoverishment. The family's financial health took a severe hit when Bartholomew Wesley was turned out of his living through the Act of Uniformity. The financial challenges continued in John's grandfather, John Wesley of Winterborn. The family apparently experienced abject poverty. We also know this earlier John Wesley entered debtor's prison. In fact, according to one author, the senior John Wesley was imprisoned four times and died relatively early.[50]

Though economic scarcity sometimes breeds meticulousness in handling money, this evidently was not the case with Samuel Wesley. This leads one to wonder whether the lack of financial resources within his father's household contributed to Samuel's demonstrated difficulties in managing money. Did the scarcity of money handicap his ability to wisely steward his resources? From history and his own admission, we know Samuel Wesley did mismanage money, thereby contributing to problems in his family. His mismanagement apparently extended to the management of his brother-in-law's, Samuel Annesley, money. Not surprisingly, this became a source of tension between the men. Susanna captured part of this tension in a letter she wrote to her brother to ameliorate the relationship between them.[51] Moreover, in another example of multigenerational transmission process, like his father before him, Samuel also wound up in debtor's prison. In fact, after Samuel's death, Susanna herself would wind up in debtor's prison because of her husband's debts.[52] This difference in financial security between the Wesley and Annesley fami-

---

49. Clarke, *Memoirs*.
50. Southey, *Rise and Progress of Methodism*.
51. Wesley, Susanna, "Letter from Epworth to her brother Samuel Annesley."
52. Clarke, *Memoirs*.

lies might have contributed to difficulties within the Epworth household. Despite her father's large brood of children, Susanna was unaccustomed to great want in her father's household; however, under her husband's roof, she experienced many years of deprivation. What consternation this must have produced in her! How troubled she must have been to see her large family in constant need!

chapter 3

Traumatic Events in the Wesley Family
Prior to John's Birth

B ESIDES THE IMPACT OF vertical stressors, horizontal or developmental stressors also shaped the Wesley household. I now turn my attention to discussing these factors in this chapter and the one that follows.
To reiterate, horizontal or developmental stressors involve those events,
which occur as the family moves across time. These events significantly
influence family atmosphere, constellation, and functioning. When considering these life events, it becomes important to pay attention to the
consequences of these changes, to what might initially appear as coincidences, and to anniversary events.[1] I now turn my attention to significant
events in the Wesley family.

Tragic Events That Influenced Wesley's Early World

According to Baker,[2] John Wesley was the fourteenth child of his parents
and the seventh child to live. John was born on June 17, 1703. He entered
a family, which had experienced great tragedy and disappointment. These
events beset the family in a relatively short space of time. This sequence of
events reads like a bad horror story in which one calamity after another
cascaded upon the innocent heads of the Epworth family. The Wesleys
could justly have sung the strains of the Hee Haw Show, "Doom, despair,
and agony on me," and not be accused of melodrama. These events largely
involved births and deaths within the family. Borrowing from family
life cycle theory, I have chosen to describe these as *entries* and *exits*.[3]

---

1. McGoldrick and Gerson, *Genograms in Family Assessment*; McGoldrick et al.,
Genograms.
2. Baker, "Investigating."
3. Carter and McGoldrick, *Family Life Cycle*; *Changing Family Lifecycle*.

Although *entries* can refer to any event, which adds members to a system (such as by marriage or adoption), I will reserve the term to denote the many births, which occurred in the Wesley family. Similarly by *exits*, I refer to the many deaths, which occurred within the Wesley nuclear and extended family. Besides these sorts of events, others such as the many tragic marriages and Hetty's escapade created havoc and adjustment problems within the family. All events, including the many entries and exits, require special adjustment within families. When a family experiences a birth, it has to broaden its boundaries to welcome the newcomer. When death occurs, the family must close ranks, wrestle with their grief, and reallocate its varied roles if it would remain viable.[4] This process is difficult enough when minor entries and exits occur. But in the Wesley family, many entries occurred and then quickly became associated with trauma because of the many stressful exits.

Entries and Exits, Tragedy and Loss (1690–1697)

I have divided the years prior to John's birth into two periods, based largely on the family's location. I include the years 1690 through 1697 in the first period. For the most part, with the exception of Samuel Wesley Junior's birth, these events occurred when the family lived at South Ormsby. Besides the many entries and exits of children, I have included two significant events, which occurred towards its end. The first event was the death of Susanna's father, Samuel Annesley. The second significant event occurring in this period involved the death of Susanna's sister, Elizabeth Dunton. The second period includes the years 1698 through 1703. According to Baker,[5] all the events in this period took place while the family resided at Epworth. Both periods produced excruciating tragedy, loss, and difficult life events, largely revolving around entries and exits from the family system. Indeed, many of the events listed in Table 3.1 involved the loss of children and other important family members.

4. Carter and McGoldrick, *Family Life Cycle; Changing Family Lifecycle.*
5. Baker, "Investigating."

TABLE 3.1. Entries and Exits, Tragedy and Loss (1690–1697)[6]

Date	Family Event
1690	Birth of Samuel Jr. while Samuel Sr. is at Sea (Samuel does not speak until he is five)
1691	Birth of Susanna, the first daughter of this name
1692	Birth of Emilia (12/31/1692?)
1693	Death and burial of daughter, Susanna (buried 4/17/1693)
1694	Birth of Jedidiah and Annesley
1695	Death and burial of Jedidiah Birth of Susanna, the second daughter with this name (the first replacement child in the family)
1696	Death and burial of Annesley Wesley Birth and crippling for life of daughter Mary Thrown out of living at South Ormsby Death of Susanna's father Dr. Samuel Annesley (12/31/1696) Disinheritance by her father
1697	Move to Epworth Death of Susanna's sister, Elizabeth Dunton (5/28/1697)

This first period began with the birth of their first child, Samuel, born in London while his father served as a naval chaplain. Samuel Junior was born at the home of Susanna's father, Dr. Samuel Annesley.[7] Following the birth of Samuel, Susanna, a daughter named after her mother, was born. She died two years later in 1693, and was buried on April 17, 1693.[8] In the meantime, the family saw another entry into the family system with the birth of the Wesley's third child, Emilia. The family saw more additions to the family in 1694 when the twins Jedidiah and Annesley were born. But tragedy would strike again as Jedidiah died in 1695 and Annesley a year later.[9] Susanna would give birth to yet another child in 1695. This was the second daughter named after her. The giving of the name Susanna to a second daughter might indicate Mrs. Wesley had not yet gotten over the loss of her first namesake. This second daughter Susanna was likely

6. Based on data from Baker, "Investigating"; Dunton, *Life and Errors*; Dallimore, *Susanna*.

7. Dallimore, *Susanna*.

8. Baker, "Investigating."

9. Ibid.

intended to carry the hopes and dreams for her dead sibling. Susanna's birth would be rapidly followed by the birth of two other girls, Mary and Hetty.[10] But even here, another tragedy befell the family—Mary Wesley was permanently crippled when a nurse dropped her. We do not know the exact nature of her injury but it was significant enough to deeply shape her identity and her self-valuing. A letter written on January 20, 1727 to her brother John depicted a person who thought little of herself. In it, she chided John for not writing to her and indicated she knew she was not one of his favorite sisters. From her perspective, nothing in her could possibly profit or benefit John. Moreover, in true mind-reading style, she expressed certainty that John held this same opinion. A little later in the letter, she remarked:

> But why should I wonder at any indifference showed to such a despicable person as myself; seeing I'm conscious there is nothing in my composition that merits esteem . . .[11]

Following Adler's ideas relative to family constellation, the letter provides some clues to the early and ongoing atmosphere in the Epworth family, at least according to Mary's perspective. In another portion of the letter, Mary indicated ". . . God has cut me off from the pleasurable parts of my life, and rendered me incapable of attracting the love of my relations . . ." In order to counter any arguments John might make to the contrary, Mary portrayed herself as having always been the jest (the butt of jokes) in the family. Further, she noted others besides her had made this observation.[12] This tragic event apparently made Mary greatly dependent on the family for necessary care. In one letter written by Martha Wesley in 1727, she highlighted Mary's continued presence at home ". . . *only because she could not get away.*"[13] (italics mine).

Besides Mary's disability, another event might have impacted the family—Samuel Wesley Jr. did not speak until he was five years old, and the family feared he was born dumb.[14] One can only imagine the consternation this event might have created in the parents. Their eldest and only surviving son, up to that point, could not speak. Given the importance of

10. Ibid.

11. Wesley, Mary, "Letter to John Wesley," January 20, 1727."

12. Ibid.

13. Welsey, Martha, "Letter to John Wesley," February 7, 1727."

14. Clarke, *Memoirs.*

sons in that day, this must have been a very painful event, especially for Samuel, his father. This reality likely gave rise to Susanna waiting until each child was five years old to teach them their letters. But other circumstances merit consideration: From 1690 onward, beginning with the birth of Samuel, Susanna became pregnant almost every year. During this seven-year period, Susanna gave birth to seven children. These births, occurring in rapid succession, must have exacted a heavy physical toll on Susanna. Besides the physical toll, Susanna and the family coped with great emotional trauma and grief including three children dying in infancy, another who was crippled permanently, and their eldest and only surviving son unable to speak for five years.

Moreover, the family experienced tremendous financial strain with the heavy weight falling on Samuel's shoulders. One letter, written while Susanna was pregnant with Emilia in 1692, almost seems callous but might reflect his heightened sense of financial pressure. Samuel wrote:

> . . . my wife's lying about last Christmas and threatening to do the same the next, and 2 children and as many servants to provide for (my wife being sickly, having had 3 or 4 touches of her rheumatism again, though we always fight it away with whey.[15]

Another letter written to Archbishop John Sharpe on May 18, 1701 also implied the financial stressors he experienced. In it he expressed his gratitude for gifts sent from the Archbishop's office, and told how he and Susanna had scrambled together six shillings to buy coals. He also acknowledged receipt of ten pounds the same day his twins, John Benjamin and Anne, were born. He wrote:

> Last night my wife brought me a few children—there are but *two* yet, a boy and a girl, and I think there are all at present. We have had four in two years and a day, three of which are living. Never came anything more like a gift from heaven than what the countess of Northampton sent by your lordship's charitable offices. Wednesday evening my wife and I clubbed and joined stocks, which came to but *six shillings,* to send for coals. Thursday morning I received the *ten pounds*: and at night my wife was delivered. Glory be to God for his unspeakable goodness![16]

In 1696, the young Wesley family was forced to leave South Ormsby. The forced transition was apparently occasioned by Samuel Wesley's ac-

15. Dallimore, *Susanna,* 35.

16. Wesley, Samuel, "Letter to Archbishop John Sharpe," May 18, 1701."

tions; by his reactionary behavior, he incurred the wrath of his benefactor and in the process hastened their exit from the parish. Some suggest the change in his benefactor's attitude toward him came about because Wesley had found the nobleman's mistress conversing in his home with Susanna and had thrown her out.[17] As a result of this event, Samuel was ejected from his home at South Ormsby. This event would prove a difficult one for the family, not only because of the loss of the living but the stress incurred by the move of a large, growing family.

Besides these intense pressures within the Wesley nuclear family, extended family events likely impacted them as well. The first such event involved the death of Dr. Samuel Annesley, Susanna's father. Coincidentally, Samuel Annesley reportedly died on Emilia Wesley's fourth birthday, December 31, 1696.[18] This coincidence might have made for a bittersweet event in the Wesley family, and might also have contributed to Susanna's connection to her eldest living daughter. According to one author, Susanna was the youngest daughter of Dr. Annesley and his most beloved child. To her, he had reportedly entrusted valuable family documents.[19] Thus, one would expect Susanna to be greatly moved by his death, and she was.[20] Other events might have compounded her pain. One author reported some degree of estrangement between Susanna and her father because of her earlier action of quitting his church and embracing the Church of England.[21] But, in addition to coping with her father's loss and any pain from estrangement, Susanna coped with another reality—her disinheritance by her beloved father. In his will, Dr. Samuel Annesley stipulated regarding the disposal of his possessions:

> My just debts being paid, I give to each of my children one shilling, and all the rest to be equally divided between my son Benjamin Annesley, my daughter Judith Annesley, and my daughter Ann Annesley whom I make my Executors of this my last Will and Testament; revoking all former, and confirming this with my hand and seal this 29 of March, 1693.[22]

17. Clarke, *Memoirs*.
18. Ibid.
19. Ibid.
20. Dallimore, *Susanna*.
21. Ibid.
22. Clarke, *Memoirs*, 299.

Giving a shilling to a child carried significance in England at that time. British law mandated an inheritance for the eldest (although it would appear this later applied to any child). The child or children left out of the will could contest the will. To prevent contesting and possible invalidation, the will's author would give a token shilling to one or more children.[23] In essence, giving a shilling to Susanna and other siblings essentially meant their disinheritance. At the minimum, it likely meant Samuel Annesley did not deem the individuals left out of the will to have significant need. But the Wesleys experienced significant financial needs. Samuel Wesley had been thrown out of his living at South Ormsby and had the expense of a move to Epworth. During this same year, they had given birth to a daughter who subsequently had been severely crippled. Given their financial destitution, this was a great loss in more ways than one. There was the psychological loss of being left out of a father's will, but also the financial loss of a likely sizable inheritance. For many years, Dr. Annesley had earned between 300–700 pounds and must have amassed quite a fortune.[24]

One other extended family event during this period deserves consideration as a potential stressor for Susanna and the Wesley family. This involved the death of Susanna's sister, Elizabeth Dunton. Elizabeth had married Samuel Wesley's former friend and publisher, John Dunton. She died on May 28, 1697 and was buried in Bunhill Fields.[25] Years later, in this same Bunhill Field, Susanna would be buried. Given their family ties and closeness in age (Elizabeth was born just prior to Susanna), Elizabeth's death must have caused some anguish for Susanna. Samuel first met Susanna when Elizabeth married John Dunton. In fact, Samuel presented the couple with a poem of ten verses to celebrate their marriage.[26] Furthermore, Samuel Wesley participated as a partner with John Dunton and Richard Sault in the Athenian Society, publisher of the Athenian Gazette, a bi-weekly publication. Besides this, Dunton had previously published Samuel Wesley's work titled "Maggots," when the latter was a nineteen year old. The two later became estranged, as indicated by words to this effect, by Dunton himself, "There is the Rector of Epworth that got his Bread by the 'Maggot' I published, has quite forgot me."[27] But

---

23. Deepti, "Traces of the Past."
24. Dallimore, *Susanna.*
25. Dallimore, *Susanna;* Dunton, *Life and Errors.*
26. Clarke, *Memoirs.*
27. Dunton, *Life and Errors,* 86.

at the time of Elizabeth's death, some connection still existed between Samuel Wesley and John Dunton. On several occasions, Dunton requested Samuel to write a eulogy and epitaph for his wife. However, Samuel did not fulfill this request until about two months after Elizabeth's death, and only partially so, having completed only the epitaph. Moreover, Susanna Wesley herself had developed a friendship with her brother-in-law, John Dunton.[28] Given this information, this must have provided yet another occasion for grief in the Epworth family.

Entries and Exits, Tragedy and Loss (1698–1703)

I chose the years 1698–1703 as another particularly difficult period for the Wesley family. This period directly led up to and culminated in the birth of John Wesley. Like the first period, many entries and exits into the family system characterized it. I have captured these events in Table 3.2.

TABLE 3.2. Entries and Exits, Tragedy and Loss (1698–1703)[29]

Date	Family Event
1698	Birth of Hetty? Birth and death of child; gender unknown
1699	Birth of twins John and Benjamin (5/16/1699)
1700	Birth and death of twins John and Benjamin Samuel's Debts—demonstrated in his letter to Dr. Sharpe 12/28/1700
1701	Birth of twins John Benjamin and Anne (5/17/1701) Death of son John Benjamin (died 12/27/1701; buried 12/30/1701)
1702	Samuel's oath following dispute with Susanna over the king (3/1/1702) Samuel separates from his marital bed Samuel leaves for London (4/5/1702) Samuel returns for 2 days (7/29/1702) Samuel leaves, vowing never to return (7/31/1702) Epworth on fire, apparently deliberately set by a servant On other side of town, Samuel told that his house was on fire and returns; First Epworth fire, 2/3 of house consumed; 400 pounds to rebuild
1703	The birth of John Wesley (6/17/1703)

This period began with the family's transition to Epworth and was closely followed by the birth of Hetty. This period also ushered in another

---

28. Clarke, *Memoirs*.

29. Based on data from Baker, "Investigating"; Dallimore, *Susanna*.

intense time of grief for the Wesley family. At least, given the author's knowledge of grief responses, the events must have caused significant bereavement in the family. Following Hetty's birth, the Wesleys faced the rapid birth and loss of four children. This surely would have been nearly unbearable for most families, as it likely was for the Wesleys. At least three of these deaths involved sons, and it is possible the fourth also was a boy, although the gender is uncertain.[30] What immense pain these losses must have unearthed in the Wesley family. Four deaths in five years! In 1698, the second child born at Epworth (Hetty being the first) soon died. Next, there followed the birth of twin boys on May 16, 1699. Following an apparent tradition for naming persons after family members, they named one boy John. Mostly likely they took the name from Samuel's own father, John Wesley of Winterborn/Whitchurch. They named the second boy Benjamin, likely after Susanna's brother of the same name. But by 1700 both boys had died. Two years after the birth of these twin boys, almost to the day, another set of twins, were born on May 17, 1701. They named the boy and the girl, John Benjamin and Anne respectively. I provide this data along with the birth and deaths of other children in a genogram in Figure 3.1.

Epworth Rectory taken by Dr. Kenneth A. Boyd (2008). Used with permission.

Several interesting coincidences appear in the birth of the twins, John Benjamin and Anne. As stated earlier, one ought to pay close attention to these coincidences as they often provide clues to the atmosphere in the family and their reactions to various life events.[31]

30. Baker, "Investigating."

31. McGoldrick and Gerson, *Genograms in Family Assessment*; McGoldrick, et al., *Genograms*.

FIGURE 3.1 The Wesley Family up to the Birth of John Wesley[32]

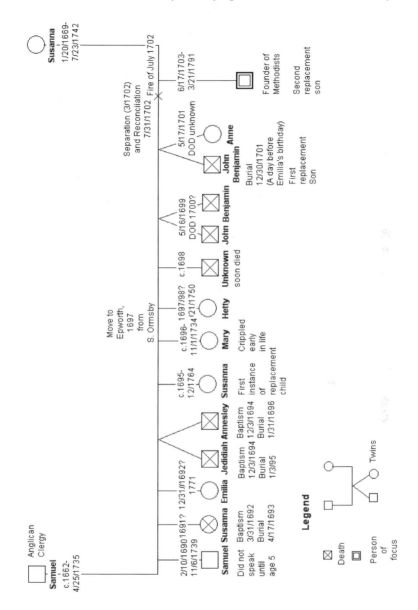

Such a coincidence occurred between the births of the two sets of twins. This latter set of twins was born almost on the anniversary of John and Benjamin's birth; John and Benjamin were born on May 16, 1699; John

32. Based on data from Baker, "Investigating."

Benjamin and Anne were born on May 17, 1701.[33] Thus, just about two years after the birth of John and Benjamin to the day, Susanna gave birth to John Benjamin and Anne. Given this reality, the births of Anne and John Benjamin's would reawaken in the parents and family, the pain attached to the loss of their previous twins. Joy over the birth of John Benjamin and Anne would be mixed with remembered grief over the loss of their two boys. It must have made for a most bittersweet event! Second, the coincidence of these births likely contributed to another interesting fact about John Benjamin: His name incorporated the names of his two dead brothers born two years previous to him, and almost on the anniversary of his birth. He must literally have appeared as a gift from God to replace his two dead brothers. No wonder they combined the two names in this new son! The family's grief and lost aspirations for the two dead boys seemed reincarnated in the birth of this son. John Benjamin became a kind of living, human memorial to two lost sons. Third, the close proximity of the birthdates of the three boys (John, Benjamin and John Benjamin) as well as the combination of the names into one son, strongly suggests the new son was a replacement child.

McGoldrick and colleagues use the term *replacement child* to describe a child born closest in time to a dead sibling. However, other definitions also appear. For example, some have used to term to refer to a child who one or both parents consciously chose to conceive in order to replace a child who died. Additionally, some have used the term to apply to a child whose family assigned this role to that child.[34] This phenomenon most often occurs when the dead child is of the same gender as the new child.[35] Somewhat surprisingly, the term has also been associated to a child born after the handicap of a live child.[36] Speaking of this phenomenon, Edwin Friedman indicated the following:

> Nature also abhors a vacuum in emotional systems. When indi-
> vidual members leave a family, whether through death, marriage,
> relocation, or a cutoff, the system will generally be quick to re-
> place the person who was lost. Whoever the replacement is, new
> child or new spouse, new in-law or new boarder, clergyman or

33. Baker, "Investigating."

34. Reid, "Clinical Research."

35. McGoldrick and Gerson, *Genograms in Family Assessment*; McGoldrick et al., *Genograms.*

36. Reid, "Clinical Research."

clergywoman, in the same generation or the next, he or she will replace in all the family triangles the person who has left. They will have grafted onto them all the expectations associated with their predecessor, an un-worked-out problems that have contributed to their predecessor's leaving (or becoming symptomatic) are likely to resurface in the new relationships. Replacement is a function of grief, and grief is always proportional to the un-worked-out residue of the relationship that was lost.[37]

These facts eminently applied to John Benjamin. Given their association, the family most likely "grafted" onto him all their expectations for John and Benjamin. These facts would also likely make him a star—a focus of attention for the family. He likely overshadowed in focus, his twin sister, Anne. But then the unspeakable happened—*this* replacement child died. Most likely, his death doubly revived all the grief and pain associated with the death of his namesakes, John and Benjamin. Indeed, his death must have compounded the grief of the family and balled it all up into one tangled mass of raw emotions. Their grief must have been unbounded! The palpable grief at John Benjamin's loss leads me to ask about the possible impact on his surviving sister, Anne. In fact, Anne seems to be one of the few surviving members of a twin born in the Wesley family, Kezia possibly being the other. How might her survival in such circumstances have influenced her? Perusal of family letters shows her as a quiet, non-demanding, almost invisible member of the Wesley family. In my judgment, she almost appeared lost in the family and, ironically, she has been lost to history.[38] Might the complicated grief at her brother's loss have contributed to shaping her in this manner? Might the family irrationally have sought to protect her for fear she too would die? Might they have failed to appropriately bond with her, fearing she might also die? Might she have grown up with survivor guilt, knowing her replacement brother had died and she, a less powerful figure, had lived? One cannot answer these questions definitively although such conclusions are supported by the literature,[39] but given the circumstances of her birth and her life, one wonders.

37. Friedman, *From Generation to Generation,* 42–43.
38. Headley, "Anne Wesley."
39. Schwab, "Parental Mourning."

Surprisingly, another coincidence relates to John Benjamin. According to Baker,[40] he was buried on December 30, 1701. The same author dates the birth of Emilia, the oldest living girl, to December 31, 1692. In short, the family buried John Benjamin almost on Emilia's birthday. One can only imagine what the coincidence of these dates must have meant for this young girl of nine years old. She already possessed a strange distinction in the family based on her birth date—her grandfather, Samuel Annesley, had died on her birthday when she was 4 years old. Perhaps these coincidences in the family's history deepened her mother's attachment to her.

The Wesleys had experienced many deaths in the family before, but nothing like what occurred during this period. This period from 1698 to 1701 produced the greatest concentration and sequential loss of children, all likely sons. Their grief must have known no bounds as one loss quickly followed another in a hopeless trail of death. McGoldrick and colleagues suggest major changes, including trauma, tends to shape families. Moreover, they recommend one pay special attention to the impact of these losses, since in these situations families experience the greatest difficulty in readjustment.[41] If this is the case, as I suspect it is, readjusting to these losses must have posed a major stumbling block to the family, and especially the parents. Giving the name John Benjamin to the new son might well represent their feeble attempt to resolve the loss of their two previous sons.

Many persons have mistakenly attached the name of this lost star, John Benjamin, to the founder of Methodism, John Wesley.[42] However, several indicate this is a mistaken view.[43] The coincidences and the nearness in birth time between John, Benjamin, and John Benjamin, which I documented, would seem to support this latter conclusion. How then does one explain the attachment of the name John Benjamin to John Wesley? How did John, himself, come to think he had been given both names but never used Benjamin?[44] As one author noted, it is likely the family became confused (it would be easy to do so with so many children and

40. Baker, "Investigating."

41. McGoldrick and Gerson, *Genograms in Family Assessment*; McGoldrick et al., *Genograms*.

42. Clarke, *Memoirs*; Moore, *Authority*; Telford, *The Letters of the Rev. John Wesley*.

43. Baker, "Investigating"; Heitzenrater, *Elusive*; Maser, *Story of John Wesley's Sisters*.

44. Clarke, *Memoirs*.

so many Johns), attaching the middle name to John Wesley.[45] However, given our present discussion, we might entertain a related hypothesis; namely, they did not call him John Benjamin simply because of confusion, but as an expression of their complicated grief. Such grief must have made for occasional lexical slippage. They had not named John Wesley by that name, but he resurrected in their memory the previously special child, John Benjamin. Now, John Wesley became the special child. One can understand their unconscious slippage. John Wesley embodied all the aspirations of three dead sons. He was in a sense, John Benjamin the Second, who like the first would carry the family's hopes and aspirations, but now for three instead of two—John, Benjamin, and John Benjamin. No wonder they might have called him John Benjamin on occasion.

I also wonder if one of the coincidences relative to the true John Benjamin might explain another reality in John Wesley's life. Wesley's sisters all seemed to have doted on him and sought him out for counsel on many matters, especially their intimate relationships. But Emilia seem particularly attached to him. Indeed, on one occasion she wrote:

> Full well you know that even from our childhood you have been selected from all our numerous family for my intimate companion, my councellor in difficulty, the dear partner of my joys and griefs. To you alone my heart lay open at all time, nor am I conscious of ever concealing my sentiment from your knowledge these many years, except in one only instance which has happened lately.[46]

I wonder if the burial of the original John Benjamin, a day short of her birthday, specially attached her to his replacement, John Wesley. This hypothesis is made more plausible because the family sometimes called him or thought about him as John Benjamin.

These hypotheses fit with the thoughts of McGoldrick and colleagues. They have noted how losses can serve to shift the focus on another family member.[47] This shift sometimes comes as a frail attempt to resolve grief (even though this might not prove entirely successful). Another possible reason for the shift is because the family reactively seeks to overprotect the survivor, or the new child. By these behaviors they hope to guard the

45. Heitzenrater, *Elusive.*

46. Wesley, E., "Letter to John Wesley," February 9, 1730."

47. McGoldrick and Gerson, *Genograms in Family Assessment*; McGoldrick et al., *Genograms.*

surviving or new child from the fate of the deceased child. Whatever the reasons, the surviving sibling, or new sibling, becomes special to the parents. Perhaps Anne Wesley might, for a while, have been a special child, being the surviving twin of her brother John Benjamin. But she was not a male. She could not embody all their hopes for dead sons. It would take another male to fully embody the others. John Wesley became this male. He alone could be the replacement child. However one thinks about such losses, one ought not to underestimate the power of such events to shape whole families in both negative and positive ways. I do not doubt this reality was true in the Wesley family. One is inclined to wonder whether the climate fostered in the family by these losses contributed to the next trauma, which would befall the Wesleys. Did these preceding events shape the family in some negative way, which made the next event more likely? This appears plausible.

The next event involved the rift, which developed between Samuel and Susanna. I shall discuss this in greater detail in chapter 4 but I present the narrative in brief at this point. Following Dallimore,[48] I believe Samuel likely used the disagreement over the king as a pretext for leaving. But what if the leaving was not simply about escaping intolerable debt and perhaps tension in the home? What if this undeniably erratic behavior on his part also derived from complicated grief, thrice compounded by the loss of sons? I do not suggest this possibility to make an excuse for Samuel. Deserting a family at such a critical time seems a callous and dastardly thing to do. However, I have seen similar responses, including desertion, in those persons struggling to resolve great grief or strong negative emotions within themselves, or in those who became overwhelmed with their life circumstances. In such cases, escape irrationally seems reasonable. In his deep distress, Samuel might have succumbed to his irrational fantasy of escape—away from the family and off to sea where he had served early in his marriage. It might have conjured up for him a time when he was relatively free from the demands of family which now pressed him. Given Samuel Wesley's apparent penchant for anger, outbursts, and, in general, impulsive behavior, this appears possible.[49] I speak about his rashness and impulsiveness for it appeared in the rash oath he made prior to withdrawing from Susanna. Earlier his impulsiveness appeared

48. Dallimore, *Susanna*.

49. Edwards, *Sons to Samuel*.

when he threw a nobleman's mistress from his home when he found her conversing with Susanna. This subsequently cost him his parish at South Ormsby.[50] Moreover, his reactive impulsivity again reared its ugly head when he forced his unwed, pregnant daughter into marriage with William Wright and summarily cut ties with her for the rest of his life.

Ironically, another family disaster, right around the time of his second leaving (see Table 3.2), put an end to the preacher's folly. This event was the fire of 1702. The fire occurred on July 31. Two days before, Samuel returned home but now he was leaving, vowing never to return. In fact, Samuel had reached the other side of town when word of the fire spread. What strange providence! Fire destroyed a home, but reunited a family! But for this fire, Samuel likely would have carried through on his plan never to return and the world would never have seen the face of one John Wesley. From this perspective, one can think the fire a strange providence—strange and strong enough to overrule the erratic behavior of an overburdened preacher.

Financial Pressures in the Wesley Family

Besides these events, the 1700's appear to have exacerbated a problem in the Wesley family, contributing to further catastrophic problems. This problem revolved around the dire financial straits of the family. The Wesleys had faced financial problems before, although at this time, the problems came to a head. These monetary problems likely issued from the many births and the growing size of the family, and events such as the disastrous fire of 1702, but there were other contributors: Samuel also incurred great debt from his attendance at several church convocations. The church convocations served as an ecclesiastical parliament tasked with regulating the affairs of the Church. Samuel had been elected to serve as a proctor, representing the Diocese of Lincoln and serving in the lower house of this body. Although this represented a high honor and indicated the esteem in which Samuel was held, it laid new financial burdens on his doorstep. This position required his presence in London for several weeks at his own expense that totaled some 50 pounds per year. Samuel continued in this position for at least three years. As a result of these extra expenses, Samuel incurred greater debt, adding further financial pressure

50. Clarke, *Memoirs*.

to his already burdened family.[51] Besides these conferences, Samuel's poor money management skills exacerbated his financial condition. This combination of circumstances placed his large, young family in dire financial straits. The 1700's apparently brought these problems to a boiling point. So thorny were his circumstances, he candidly disclosed his situation to Archbishop Sharpe in a letter written on December 28, 1700:

> I must own I was ashamed, when at Bishop Thorp, to confess that I was three hundred pounds in debt, when I had a living of which I have made two hundred pounds per annum, though I could hardly let it now for eightscore. I doubt not but one reason of my being sunk so far is, my not understanding worldly affairs; and my aversion to law, which my people have always known but too well. But I think I can give a tolerable account of my affairs, and satisfy any equal judge that a better husband than myself might have been in debt, though, perhaps, not so deeply, had he been in the same circumstances, and met with the same misfortunes.[52]

Wesley continued the letter by providing specific details relative to his debts including those incurred from the convocations. Surprisingly, he added these expenses to prior debt while his family at home lived in dire need.[53] In fact, Samuel incurred so much debt, he was imprisoned for debt for three months in the latter part of 1705, returning home by Christmas. But Samuel Wesley's money problems did not end there. In fact, his problems continued for the rest of his life. These problems created lasting hardships for the entire family. It heaped on them significant privations, especially on the girls in the family. But, it also appears to have produced lasting impact on the family atmosphere and psyche, creating an apparent hostility, especially among the girls, notably Emilia. She highlighted these ongoing difficulties and repercussions in a letter written to John in April 17, 1725. In it she noted:

> I know not when we have had so good a year, both at Wroote and at Epworth, as this year; but instead of saving anything to clothe my sister or myself, we are just where we were. A noble crop has almost gone, beside Epworth living, to pay some part of those infinite debts my father has run into, which are so many, that were he to save 50 (pounds) a year, he would not be clear in the world this

51. Clarke, *Memoirs*; Dallimore, *Susanna*.

52. Clarke, *Memoirs*, 159–60.

53. Edwards, *Family Circle*.

seven years. One thing I warn you of: let not my giving you this account be any hindrance to your affairs. If you want assistance in any case, my father is as able to give it now as any time these last ten years; nor shall we be ever the poorer for it.[54]

In the same letter she clearly linked the family's financial troubles to her father's attendance at the church's convocations, noting his absence for seven winters:

> . . . but after we were gotten into our house and all the family were settled, in about a year's time, I began to find out we were ruined, then came on London journeys, convocations of blessed memory, that for seven winters my father was at London and we at home in intolerable want and affliction, then I learnt what it was to seek money and bread seldom having any without such hardships in getting it . . . "

Such were the many difficult circumstances, which beset the Epworth family prior to the birth of John Wesley. These events and circumstances surely influenced the Wesley family constellation in terms of its physical ramifications as well as the psychological and emotional atmosphere present in the family. As we saw in a previous chapter, family constellation shapes identities of the persons within the family. They surely must have partly shaped John Wesley's identity and the sort of person he became. Wesley implies as much when he indicated the implications his parents' rift and reunion held for his personal biography. As I suggested earlier, events within the family carved out for him a central role; he became the replacement child who would fulfill the lost dreams and potential of three dead sons. But he also arrived in a family burdened down by grief, poverty, and deeply pained by many unpredictable traumas. One can only imagine the climate these circumstances fostered in the Wesley home. Into this emotional and financially stricken cauldron, John Wesley was born.

54. Welsey, E., "Letter to John Wesley," April 7, 1725."

chapter 4

Wesley's Early Recollections
and Family Context

"CONTEXT IS EVERYTHING!" DR. Robert Lyon, one of my former seminary professors often stated this to his students. He served Asbury Theological Seminary as a professor of New Testament and spoke these words in the context of biblical interpretation. To understand and do justice to the biblical text, he emphasized the need to decipher the context in which words were spoken. One needed to understand the immediate context as well as the historical and cultural background from which the words derived. Only in understanding these elements of the biblical passage, could one truly come to discern its intent and meaning. Anything else would represent proof texting and presenting a message far different than that intended by the biblical writer. Of course, Dr. Lyon was right. In order to understand scripture, "context is everything!"

But this principle of biblical interpretation applies not only to ancient texts; it also applies to human texts. Strangely enough, one cannot fully understand people apart from their context. For this reason, when conducting therapy it becomes necessary to collect social and historical information, including family experiences. Without this background information, one arrives at a partially true and sometimes partially distorted view of the individual. Many writers in the therapy field make this point. For example, in his famed text, *The Skilled Helper*, Gerard Egan[1] indicated the need for fully developed helpers to inculcate a people in systems framework. For Egan, helping professionals need to understand the contexts which shaped persons if they are to make sense of their lives and world. As part of this concept, Egan indicated the need to understand clients in the various settings of their lives as well as comprehend the different ways such settings influenced their behavior. "Context is everything!"

1. Egan, *Skilled Helper*.

In this chapter, I continue my discussion of the Wesley family context. In particular, I pay attention to significant events, which shaped members of the Wesley family, especially our person of focus, John Wesley.

Family Events Which Influenced John Wesley

In chapter 1, I indicated the relevance of Alfred Adler's concept of *Early Recollections* for understanding John Wesley. In this chapter I shall devote the greater attention to two key events, which influenced his life. These two events clearly fit into Adler's understanding of *Early Recollections*. They included the rupture between his parents and their subsequent separation and reunion. Significantly, Wesley connected this event with another recollection, the haunting of the family by Old Jeffrey. Wesley did not directly experience this latter event since he was away at school. However, his sisters provided the details of the story and this evidently sparked enough interest in him to provide his own account of the event.[2] The second event was the devastating fire of 1709 from which he and several other siblings were saved. As I indicated in chapter 1, *Early Recollections* provide a window on the individual's world, providing valuable insights into what makes them tick. They also provide clues to their values and strived for goals. These two events served such purposes in John Wesley's life. As we will see, both events played a significant role in Wesley's understanding of himself. His parent's separation and reunion evidently carried meaning for the way he understood his life and history. In addition, the fire of 1709 apparently influenced his sense of purpose and mission as evidenced in his co-opting the phrase "a brand pluck'd from the burning" to capture his sense of God's purpose in his life. One can also view these early recollections from the prism of McGoldrick's idea of horizontal family stressors. That is, these recollected events represented developmental, non-normative events, which likely served to create heightened stress within the family system. In particular, Samuel's desertion of his family helped instill a sense of insecurity and distrust in those who experienced the event, especially in Susanna and his daughters. Although I have previously discussed the significant loss of children and Wesley's status as replacement child, I shall revisit this discussion in brief, investigating it from the perspective of early recollections.

---

2. Clarke, *Memoirs*; Maser, *Story of John Wesley's Sisters*.

But the story of the shaping of John Wesley's life would be incomplete if I did not mention the feminine world in which he was reared. From personal experience I know this can carry significant influence. My earliest memory revolved around growing up in a world of women, my grandmother, and later my mother, and a sister on either side of me. I learned to do many of the things they did, as my family did not make distinctions between chores for boys and girls. I learned early to cook and clean, to starch, iron, and sew clothing. I still enjoy doing these activities to some degree. Having also grown up in a feminine world and knowing some of the ways in which it impacted me, I cannot imagine Wesley being left untouched. I now turn my attention to discussing these early recollections events and the early feminine world of John Wesley.

Early Recollections: The Rupture and Reunion of His Parents

In his *Memoirs of the Wesley Family*, eminent Wesley historian, Adam Clarke,[3] reported a significant early recollection, which John Wesley himself related. The reported story illustrates for us the power of family events for shaping individuals. Moreover, the event and its recollection demonstrate how such occurrences can wield power over the individual's identity and life trajectory. These events possess power even when they occurred prior to one's birth. To recall the language of Adler, recollections possess the power to shape identity, one's lifestyle, and the goals for which they believe they should strive.[4] The rupture and reunion of his parents exerted such power on John's identity, providing for him an explanatory clue to his life. We see this implied in words Wesley reportedly told Clarke:

> "Were I," said he, "to write my own life, I should begin it *before I was born*, merely for the purpose of mentioning a disagreement between my father and mother. 'Sukey,' said my father to my mother, one day, after family prayers, 'why did you not say *amen* this morning to the prayer for the king?' 'Because,' said she, 'I do not believe the prince of Orange to be king.' 'If that be the case,' said he, ' you and I must part; for if we have two kings, we must have two beds.' My mother was inflexible. My father went immediately to his study; and, after spending some time with himself, set out for London, where, being *convocation man* for the diocese

3. Clarke, *Memoirs*.

4. Adler, *Science of Living; Significance; Individual Psychology*.

of Lincoln, he remained without visiting his own house for the remainder of the year. On March 8th in the following year, 1702, King William died; and as both my father and mother were agreed as to the legitimacy of Queen Anne's title, the cause of their misunderstanding ceased. My father returned for Epworth, and conjugal harmony was restored."[5]

The British newspaper, the Manchester Guardian, reported this event and its consequences in a sequence of articles written on July 2 and July 3, 1953. Those articles were respectively titled *John Wesley's Parents: I—Their Quarrel over and "Amen,"* and *John Wesley's Parents II—Fire and Reconciliation.*[6] Together these articles detailed, through the use of primary documents, the unfolding of the events involved in the estrangement and reconciliation of his Wesley's parents. Given the details gleaned from the primary documents, it appears, following Susanna's refusal to say amen, Samuel deserted his wife's bed, even though he stayed at home for a while. Susanna seemed to exhibit a different spirit than Samuel in that she was willing to accompany him to communion in spite of his behavior. Susanna reported the sequence of events to Lady Yarborough in the following language:

> . . . You advise me to continue with my husband, and God knows how gladly I would do it, but there, there is my supreme affliction, he will not live with me. 'Tis but a little while since he one evening observed in our family prayers that I did not say Amen to his prayer for KW [King William] as I usually do to all others; upon which he retired to his study, and calling me to him asked the reason of my not saying Amen to the prayer. I was a little surprised at the question and don't know well what I answered, but too well I remember what followed: he immediately kneeled down and imprecated the divine vengeance upon himself and all his posterity if ever he touched me more or came into a bed with me before I had begged God's pardon and his for not saying Amen to prayer for the king.[7]

Samuel eventually deserted the family and left for London at Easter as indicated by the following portion of the same letter to Lady Yarborough:

---

5. Clarke, *Memoirs*, 165–66.

6. *Manchester Guardian*, July 2, 1953; July 3, 1953.

7. *Manchester Guardian*, July 2, 1953, 8.

> I've represent as long as I could be heard the sin of the oath and the ill consequences of it to my master, but he cannot be convinced he has done ill, nor does the present change in state [the king's death on March 8] make any alteration in his mind . . . He is for London at Easter where he designs to try if he can get a chaplain's place in a man of war. [a naval vessel][8]

Samuel apparently left and returned on two occasions. On the second occasion, he had traveled as far as the other side of town before he received the news of a fire at his home, to which he hastily returned. This was the first of two devastating fires the family experienced. This fire was reputedly set by one of the servants and devastated two-thirds of the house. This plunged the family into further debt for its repair. However, the event ended Samuel's desertion. According to Dallimore, Samuel used the fire to justify staying at home while yet claiming he had kept his oath.[9]

Wesley claimed marital bliss was restored upon his father's return. Given the traumatic nature of this event, a blissful outcome is highly unlikely. As a result, some writers have disputed this fairy tale ending.[10] To the contrary, the correspondence discussed earlier revealed intense conflict and agony in Susanna.[11] In fact, Dallimore[12] claimed this event impacted Samuel and his family in two significant ways: First, Susanna's attitude to him would change to a great measure. As evidenced by her letter to Lady Yarborough, Samuel's desertion proved an exceedingly traumatic event for her. Having her trust betrayed in such a dramatic way, it is unlikely she would still feel the same way toward him. One must also wonder about the impact upon the children present in the home at the time of his desertion. This likely influenced them greatly. It might have impacted the Wesley girls the greatest, especially given any identification with their mother. Their letters often betrayed their struggle with their father and his decision, especially his perceived deficiencies in providing for his family. Emilia, who was around 9 years old at the time of her father's desertion, seemed to experience some of the greatest struggles. I characterize her as the chief repository of painful family events. As noted earlier, in one of her numerous letters to John, written in April 1725, she

8. *Manchester Guardian*, July 2, 1953, 8.

9. Dallimore, *Susanna*.

10. Dallimore, *Susanna*; Rack, *Reasonable Enthusiast*.

11. Rack, *Reasonable Enthusiast*.

12. Dallimore, *Susanna*.

related some of the family events in vivid detail, even recalling the fire of 1709 when she was 14. She also referenced her father's convocations and the deprivations this placed on the family.[13] Although I could find no other reference to the parental separation other than that recorded by John Wesley, one wonders if part of their frustration proceeded not only from the circumstances they experienced, but also from past memories of their trauma and desertion (at least in Emilia's case). Their father's desertion, deeply seared into their consciousness, must have remained one of the most significant traumatic events they experienced. Having some knowledge of human nature, I cannot imagine it not impacting them deeply. Second, the desertion of his family likely hindered him from rising within the hierarchy of the church. Up to this time, Samuel ostensibly had achieved a high regard in the church, having been elected to serve as proctor to the convocation of the Church of England on more than one occasion. But now the word was out about his actions, for Susanna had corresponded with Bishop Hickes about the matter.[14]

This unfortunate event seems important for several reasons. First, it illustrates well how issues at the macro level (the question regarding the legitimacy of King William's right to the throne) can influence events at the micro level, in this case, the family level. According to an earlier discussion, this event fits Carter and McGoldrick's definition of a family stressor.[15] It was at once a vertical stressor, related as it was to a national and political issue, as well as a horizontal (developmental) stressor on the family. Thus, political turmoil and differences over the rightful king ostensibly forged a rupture in the Epworth family. I say ostensibly because Dallimore[16] believed Samuel Wesley used the prayer to the king as a pretext for leaving. After 12 years of marriage, Dallimore reasoned Samuel must have long noticed Susanna's refusal to say amen to the king. The difference on this occasion revolved around the death of Queen Mary. Samuel had sought and gained her goodwill, but with her death, he now feared if his wife's refusal to say amen to the king became known, it would curtail his hopes of securing preferment in the church.[17] Ironically, his own rash actions de-

13. Welsey, E., "Letter to John Wesley," April 7, 1725."

14. Walmsley, "John Wesley's Parents"; Dallimore, *Susanna*.

15. Carter and McGoldrick, *Family Life Cycle; Changing Family Lifecycle*.

16. Dallimore, *Susanna*.

17. Ibid.

stroyed his chances of rising in the church. At any rate, whether for real or by pretext, politics played a role in the Wesley's separation. In this regard, their separation would not be unlike a rift developing in an American family because one spouse espoused allegiance to the Republican Party while the other expressed staunch support for the Democratic Party. It would be akin to Mary Matalin and James Carville, a married couple on opposite extremes of the political spectrum, parting because of their different views. Unlike them, Samuel was not able to tolerate the political difference and deserted his wife and his six young children.

Second, the event also provides a good illustration of two persons living at the opposite ends of self-differentiation. It clearly indicates an individuation problem within his parent's marriage. Samuel Wesley's famous words to Susanna: "... *if we have two kings, we must have two beds,*" represents a classic statement of an undifferentiated person. To live with her, he must have her conform exactly to his political views. In other words, he strove for a sameness of views relative to the burning political question; he sought to forge a kind of political symbiosis with his wife. Perhaps his need for her conformity represented an unspoken, implicit expectation of his spouse, now made explicit at a critical time in their family life cycle and political history. Not finding this sameness of view regarding the rightful king, he acted in an emotionally reactive manner and deserted his struggling family. Samuel's actions indicate both intrapsychic and interpersonal problems in self-differentiation. His cutoff from Susanna and his family clearly illustrate problems in his relationship with Susanna deriving from their difference of opinion. In terms of intrapsychic differentiation, his emotions and reason seemed fused. How else does one explain Samuel's behavior? How does one explain deserting a wife and six children under the age of twelve? What rationale can one provide for such action by an apparently sane clergyman of the Church of England over a matter like saying "Amen" to a prayer for the king? His behavior defies explanation.

Just recently, I met a female friend of one of my sons. I had not seen her for sometime and she was pregnant when I saw her. In our conversation, she told me of a recent desertion by her husband, even though she was five months pregnant. When my son heard this tale of his friend, he wondered what kind of man would desert his wife, especially when she carried his child. His question spurs the same response in me, for Samuel's desertion is similar, though far worse. He deserted a wife and six small children. I can only offer one possible explanation: Samuel had lost all logic and reasoned from the standpoint of reactive emotions. His actions also betrayed his difficulty dealing with emotional closeness when tension existed in the relationship. Persons functioning at a low level of differentiation tend to do exactly what Samuel did; emotionally cut-off from the offending person.[18]

Significantly, Susanna appears to have arrived at a higher level of differentiation than Samuel. She showed willingness to allow him his opinions, but he did not reciprocate. Her words to Lady Yarborough, ". . . that since I'm willing to let him quietly enjoy his opinions, he ought not to deprive me of my little liberty of conscience,"[19] showed her calm reasoning of the situation, unclouded by anxiety. It proved her a highly differentiated individual who displayed a healthy combination of emotion and reason in her decision-making.[20] She was able to acknowledge her emotions, but not allow them to cloud her reasoning, thereby prompting an emotional reaction. The same could not be said for Samuel. His judgment, clouded by impulsive emotions, clearly evidenced itself. The incident provided a clear picture of a highly differentiated woman who must struggle with a man living at a low level of differentiation.

Samuel's desertion of his family also provides illustration of another Bowen concept, namely emotional cut-off or fugue.[21] In this case, we see both physical and emotional distancing. Removing his self from her bed and deserting the family involved elements of both emotional and physical distancing. Triangulation also appears in the incident. In her attempts to redress the wrong, Susanna wrote to both Lady Yarborough and Bishop Hickes. It also appeared Samuel contacted Bishop John Sharpe over the matter.[22]

Perhaps the greatest significance of the event involves its relationship to John Wesley. In a sense, Wesley was not simply a brand plucked from the Epworth Fire of 1709,[23] he was also birthed from the fire of 1702. One wonders but for this fire, whether Samuel would have returned to his family or whether he would have followed his plans to become a chaplain

18. Blessing, "Murray Bowen's"; Bowen, "Toward the Differentiation"; *Family Therapy.*

19. Dallimore, *Susanna*, 48.

20. Blessing, "Murray Bowen's."

21. Blessing, "Murray Bowen's"; Bowen, *Family Therapy*; Nichols, *Family Therapy*; Nichols and Schwartz, *Family Therapy*; Skowron, "Differentiation of Self."

22. Dallimore, *Susanna.*

23. Clarke, *Memoirs.*

aboard a naval vessel. In less than a year following the first fire, his parent's reunion birthed John Wesley, the crowning product of his parents' reconciliation. These circumstances likely helped carved out a special place for John Wesley in the Epworth household. As I will demonstrate in a later chapter, Wesley became a special and central figure in the family. Even if one debates John Wesley's special place in the family, from his own mouth we knew his parents' separation played a signal role in his biography. Wesley did not tell us why he would begin his autobiography with the separation of his parents but he evidently thought it possessed a special connection to his identity and life. The separation and reunion appeared an early recollection, which would, in some unspoken fashion, influence and shape his life. Neither did Wesley tell us how he came into possession of the story, but we can make plausible guesses. The event likely became resident in the family memory, even if left largely unspoken; for all intent, it became a negative family event, which would partly define the family's identity. Although I doubt this event was constantly rehearsed, I suspect it might have come up at some time even if not from Samuel or Susanna (which I doubt). Perhaps the older children such as Samuel Jr., Emilia, Susanna, or Hetty, who had lived through this trauma, might have related it at some time. The event might even have become embedded in the memory of Samuel's parishioners at Epworth and related in the community. After all, Samuel had not only deserted his family, he had also abandoned his parishioners.

John Wesley thought his father's desertion of his wife and children a serious error. Indeed, he perceived the visitation of Old Jeffrey as the punishment meted out by God on Samuel for his desertion. Old Jeffrey was the supposed ghost who haunted the Wesley family in the latter part of 1715 and the beginning of 1716.[24] Wesley evidently made this association because the ghost first appeared when the family prayed for the king during family prayers. We see the association of these two events in Wesley's own words:

> At six in the evening, he had family-prayers, as usual. When he began the prayer for the King, a knocking began all round the room; and a thundering knock attended the Amen. The same was heard from this time every morning and evening, while the prayer for the King was repeated. As both my father and mother are now at rest, and incapable of being pained thereby, I think it my duty

24. Ibid.

to furnish the serious reader with a key to this circumstance. The year before King William died, my father observed my mother did not say Amen to the prayer for the King. She said she could not; for she did not believe the Prince of Orange was King. He vowed he would never cohabit with her till she did. He then took his horse, and rode away; nor did she hear anything of him for a twelvemonth. He then came back, and lived with her as before. But I fear his vow was not forgotten before God.[25]

Early Recollections: A Brand Plucked from the Fire

The second Epworth fire of 1709 proved another significant early recollection, which greatly influenced Wesley's life. The fire occurred on February 9, 1709 and destroyed the rectory including furniture, books, and manuscripts.[26] The fire came at an unfortunate time for many reasons. Among these was Susanna's pregnancy with her nineteenth child, the tenth who lived. At the time of the fire, she was some eight months pregnant, and gave birth to Kezia one month after the fire.[27] The fire apparently started near midnight. Hetty Wesley was the first who became aware of the impending calamity when sparks from the roof fell on her feet. She wisely alerted her parents. Samuel had already heard the cry of "fire!" and soon discovered the alarm pertained to his own home. He quickly roused his family and facilitated their escape by varied avenues. Though big with child, Susanna braved the flames, and escaped naked but not without consequences; in the process, she had scorched her hands and feet. Then it was discovered, not everyone had escaped,—John yet remained in the house. Alerted by his cry, Samuel attempted to rescue John but could not because the flames had already engulfed the stairs, impeding any chance of rescue. Resigned to the tragedy, Samuel knelt in prayer and committed John's soul to God.[28] At this point in the story, John Wesley himself picked up his miraculous rescue:

> "I believe," observes Mr. John Wesley, "it was just at that time I waked; for I did not cry as they imagined, unless it was afterward. I remember all the circumstances as distinctly as though it were but yesterday. Seeing the room was very light, I called to the maid to

25. Jackson, "The Works," Vol. 13, 504.

26. Clarke, *Memoirs*; Edwards, *Family Circle*.

27. Telford, *The Life of John Wesley*.

28. Clarke, *Memoirs*; Heitzenrater, *Elusive*.

take me up. But none answering, I put my head out of the curtains, and saw streaks of fire on the top of the room. I got up and ran to the door, but could get no further, all the door beyond it being in a blaze. I then climbed up on a chest, which stood near the window: one in the yard saw me, and proposed running to fetch a ladder. Another answered, 'there will not be time; but I have thought of another expedient. Here I will fix myself against the wall; lift a light man, and set him upon my shoulders.' They did so; and he took me out of the window. Just then the whole roof fell in; but it fell inward, or we had all been crushed at once. When they bought me into the house where my father was, he cried out, 'Come, neighbors, let us kneel down; let us give thanks to God! He has given me all my eight children; let the house go; I am rich enough.' The next day as he was walking in the garden and surveying the ruins of the house, he picked up a part of a leaf of his Polyglot Bible, on which just those words were legible: Vade; vende omneia quae habes, et attolle crucem et sequere me. 'Go; sell all that thou hast; and take up thy cross, and follow me.'"[29]

From the accounts given above, other members of the family, besides John Wesley, were saved from the fire. According to Heitzenrater,[30] the narratives found in Susanna's and John's accounts highlighted the saving of all the children. Later, however, the focus of the fire shifted to John Wesley, himself. Moreover, by 1737, John adopted the phrase "a brand plucked out of the burning," in reference to himself.

This fire significantly impacted the family. It placed enormous financial burdens on Samuel Wesley for rebuilding the rectory, adding to already onerous obligations. Additionally, the fire separated the family; many of the children were farmed out to the homes of friends and relatives.[31] Besides this, as one might expect, an enormous emotional impact ensued. Such sentiments appeared in a letter Susanna wrote to her son, Samuel, in October of 1709. She wrote:

Dear Samy,

Tho nothing in the world could ever make me forget you or prevent my having the tenderest regard for ye happiness, and concern for ye immortal soul; yet my mind has bin so terribly shock'ed by our late misfortunes, that tho I cannot say I never had leisure, yet

29. Clarke, *Memoirs*, 344–45.
30. Heitzenrater, *Elusive*.
31. Clarke, *Memoirs*; Edwards, *Family Circle*.

I couldn't dispose myself to write to ye. A long series of adverse
fortunes had before inclin'd me to a too melancholy temper, but
this most strange and surprising accident attended by too many
calamitous circumstances gave my soul so strong a bent to extreme
sadness that I haven't bin able to recover myself . . . but have bin
as one dead to ye world, uncapable (sic) of enjoying any of those
comforts . . . God in his mercy hath yet left me."[32]

Besides the impact of the fire, Susanna made reference to "a long
series of adverse fortunes," disposing her to melancholy. Susanna's language evokes images of a pile up of negative events in the family. These
had taken an emotional toll on her, apparently bringing her to depression. Besides these events, one would recall her pregnancy during the
fire and giving birth a month after the fire.[33] Who then could blame her
for the melancholy evident in this letter to Samuel? Furthermore, the
event apparently took its emotional toll on other family members. It evidently impacted Emilia, the oldest girl at home at the time. In fact, when
the children were scattered, Emilia remained at home with her mother.
Emilia recalled this and other events in a letter written to John in 1725. In
this letter cited earlier, she spoke about her growing reality of the family's
ruin. As the reader might recall, she attributed much of this to her father's
choices and behaviors. She indicated how the family subsisted on the bare
necessities, finding it difficult to get money and bread without great effort. In the midst of this deprivation, and the family's "intolerable want
and affliction," her father continued his journeys to London to church
convocations.[34]

But beyond the impact of individuals and the family as a whole, the
Epworth fire of 1709 bore personal significance for John Wesley, at least
in the mind of Susanna. She called him "the brand plucked from the fire,"
and believed God had saved him for a special work, and from that time
she gave him special attention.[35] This "specialness" of John came through
in Susanna's diary entry:

I do intend to be more particularly careful of the soul of this child,
that Thou hast so mercifully provided for, than ever I have been,

32. Wesley, Susanna, "Letter from Epworth," October 11, 1709.

33. Telford, *The Life of John Wesley*.

34. Welsey, E., "Letter to John Wesley," April 7, 1725.

35. Abelove, *Evangelist of Desire*; Collins, *A Real Christian*; Ethridge, *Strange Fire*;
Telford, *The Life of John Wesley*.

that I may do my endeavour to instil into his mind the principles
of Thy true religion and virtue. Lord, give me grace to do it sin-
cerely and prudently, and bless my attempts with good success.[36]

Whether John came to believe in his own special destiny, is a matter
of debate. In response to one Mr. Badcock's claim of his early sense of special destiny, John Wesley wrote a rebuttal. This was initially printed in the
Gentleman's Magazine and reprinted in the Armenian magazine in 1784.
In it, Wesley proclaimed: "Indeed not I; I never said so. I am guiltless in
this matter."[37] He then traced his vocational journey from the age of 23
or 24 when he intended to spend the rest of his days seeking truth within
academia. He continued by speaking about his time spent as his father's
curate at Wroote and then the circumstances, which led to his missionary
endeavor in Georgia. Even after his return from Georgia, Wesley still appeared bent on an academic career as reflected in this statement:

> At my return, I was more than ever determined to lay my bones
> at Oxford. But I was insensibly led, without any previous plan or
> design, to preach first in many of the churches in London, then in
> more public places; afterwards in Bristol, Kingswood, Newcastle,
> and throughout Great Britain and Ireland. Therefore all that Mr.
> Badcock adds, of the incidents that "gave additional force" to an
> impression that never existed, is very ingenious, yet is in truth a
> castle in the air.[38]

Curnock[39] believed John Wesley thought himself plucked by a
special providence in more than one sense. The phrase took on special
significance for him and he used it often and not just verbally. For example, Curnock noted the inscription of the phrase on the manuscript
account of Miss Sophy. Moreover, According to Curnock, Wesley used
it as a legend and paired it with a drawing of a burning house on one of
the engraved portraits published during his life.[40] Thus, Wesley used the
phrase to illustrate his salvation from the fire for a special purpose. He
also employed it as a metaphor for escape from other difficult situations.
For example, Wesley used it to describe his narrow escape from entering

36. Telford, *The Life of John Wesley*, 19–20.

37. Heitzenrater, *Elusive*, 43.

38. Ibid.

39. Curnock, "The Journal."

40. Curnock, "The Journal," Vol.1.

into a committed relationship with Sophy Hopkey. We find this in his diary entry for March 7, 1737. On that day he made another contact with Sophy and appeared on the verge of forgetting his resolve not to marry. However, before he could break his resolve, Mr. Causton, Sophy's uncle by marriage, interrupted them. Having experienced such a close shave, Wesley wrote: "So I was once more 'snatched as a brand out of the fire.'"[41]

In fact, this statement came not only to define Wesley but also became a favorite phrase used by early Methodists to describe their conversion experience. In a conversation with Brian Yeich, who is conducting doctoral research on conversion narratives, I discovered the phrase "a brand plucked from the fire," occurred frequently among the early Methodists.[42] An example of this can be found in a letter written by Catherine Gilbert to Charles Wesley in 1740 in which she noted: "I am pluckt as a firebrand out of the fire" to describe her salvation experience.[43] When I spoke to Dr. Yeich, I immediately recognized the phrase as one employed by John Wesley. Apparently, his converts adopted his language relative to his escape from the Epworth fire of 1709 as a way of describing their salvation experience. Their use of this phrase implies their common knowledge of its significance for Wesley. Because of reverence for him, they likely desired to identify with him, even in small matters. The use of this phrase provided an opportunity for them to identify their salvation experience with his escape metaphor.

Early Recollections: The Loss of Children and Wesley as Replacement Child

In the previous chapter, I discussed the significant loss of children, especially the loss of sons and how these events placed John Wesley in the role of replacement child. I revisit the topic here from the perspective of early recollections. Given this perspective, these events would have become embedded in the Wesleys' memory, shaping their individual identities and functioning. This holds true because such events often become uniquely personal for each person in the family. At the same time, such events affect the family as a corporate body.[44] But, though such events

---

41. Ibid, 328.

42. Yeich, *Conversation on John Wesley.*

43. Gilbert, "Catherine Gilbert to Charles Wesley."

44. Schwab, "Parental Mourning."

might remain dormant for a while, they rarely remain so. In a few instances and at a later date, those early, painful memories would live again in a new child given an old name. The new child would in a sense become a living memorial to the dead sibling. In Wesley's case, he became a living memorial to three dead sons (see figure 4.1).

FIGURE 4.1 Deaths Prior to John Wesley's Birth[45]

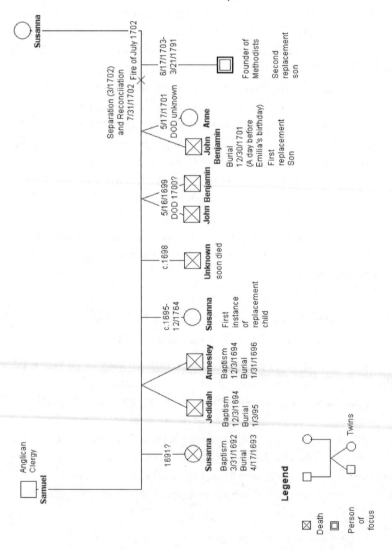

This phenomenon likely carries significance for several reasons, although I will only mention a few. First, the child who died normally becomes idealized, sometimes posing difficulties for the replacement child in measuring up.[46] Second, such events can help curtail the identity of the replacement child in that this person is expected to assume the identity of the deceased child. Furthermore, being reared in the shadow of a deceased child might lead to an invalidation of the replacement child's identity.[47] In this sense, the replacement child is almost not his or her own person, but instead has had his or her identity co-opted by the dead child. In fact, such an event can become etched upon the inner world of the replacement child, serving as a ". . . concrete reminder of the loss and as an undigested experience within the mother-child relationship."[48] Perhaps this shared experience of mother and child partly explains the relationship that existed between Susanna and John Wesley. Third, as indicated earlier, John's status contributed to a sense of specialness about John Wesley. According to McGoldrick and colleagues, circumstances such as attended John Wesley's birth endow the child with some heightened degree of specialness. Sometimes this specialness contributes to great intensity generated in the relationship between the child and the parents.[49] McGoldrick and colleagues demonstrated this specialness through persons such as Geraldine Ferraro who was named for her dead sibling Gerald.[50] Apparently, such circumstances might predispose an individual to a sense of uniqueness and destiny as demonstrated in Wesley's case.[51] Additionally, these circumstances possess significant power to shape the bearer of the name.

Sometime ago, I read a story in our local newspaper, which demonstrated this phenomenon and its power to shape one's life and the sense of specialness. The story involved Kelenna Azubuike, a basketball player at the University of Kentucky. In his early teens, his parents related to him a tale of an older brother who, as a baby, had suffocated in his sleep. That child also bore the name Kelenna. The death of this child crushed

46. Schwab, "Parental Mourning."

47. Ibid.

48. Reid, "Clinical Research," 209.

49. McGoldrick and Gerson, *Genograms in Family Assessment*; McGoldrick, et al., *Genograms*.

50. Ibid.

51. Moore, *Authority*.

his mother, leading to nightly tears. One night, she had a dream in which God promised to bring the baby back and put his blessings on him. When the UK basketball player was born, his parents also named him Kelenna. Upon first hearing the story, Kelenna literally saw his life as a born again experience: "So I was born twice . . . I'm the second version of me. The first one is dead." Kelenna Azubuike said the thought made him feel special. In fact, his mother told him he was special because God had given her the baby back.[52] Here, one sees some of the themes mentioned earlier such as the implications for identity in that Kelenna seems to identify almost completely with his dead brother. Second, one sees the uniqueness of the relationship between the mother and child, and third, the air of specialness seems almost palpable in the account. Such is the impact and the specialness attributed to a replacement child. Such events invariably provide drive and motivation to the person who lives. I suspect some of the drive and goal-driven behavior evident in John Wesley might have sprung from this sense of living his life for four persons (himself and three brothers). Having been named John and believing he also carried the name Benjamin, he bore them as a memorial, motivation, and possibly a burden. Besides, he also bore the name John in memory of his grandfather, the heroic John Wesley of Winterborn. What powerful motivations for drive and determination!

Fourth, although replacement children can become discouraged and fail to live up to expectations, some seem to rise to lofty levels of achievement. Perhaps they are driven by the sense of being unique and being a person of destiny. Because they have lived with the idea that their lives belong to another, sacrifice becomes a common way of being and a source for striving. Whatever inspires their achievement, many persons born in these circumstances achieve on a grand scale. McGoldrick and colleagues listed such luminaries F. Scott Fitzgerald, Sigmund Freud, Henry Ford, Carl Jung, Harry Stack Sullivan, Beethoven, and Ben Franklin.[53] We can add the venerable name of John Wesley to this pantheon of great achievers. No doubt, his drive and achievement was partly fueled by the early and abiding recollection of living his life for many brothers.

52. Tipton, "Blessed Child."

53. McGoldrick and Gerson, *Genograms in Family Assessment*; McGoldrick, et al., *Genograms*.

The Feminine World of Wesley

Besides the recollected events, another circumstance in the family likely influenced John Wesley's life and ministry in profound ways. This element of his early family environment likely partly accounts for his lifelong contact and correspondence with many women. Malwyn Edwards[54] in *"My Dear Sister,"* documented some of these relationships. Furthermore, he noted Wesley's great fondness for women and how he corresponded with them three times as much as he did to men, a pattern which continued across his life. In a similar vein, Moore[55] noted John Wesley's love of women's company and attributed this to his early experiences in his home. Further, he surmised the company of women afforded Wesley intimacy without the taint of passion or desire. We likely view this familiarity with many women in a negative light, given our current and appropriate concerns about the prevalence of sexual misconduct. But, even if one sets aside this issue (and in Wesley's case, one should), a consideration of the repercussions in Wesley's life gives one cause for concern. Collins' study of Wesley's life described his close acquaintance with women as a contributing factor in the breakdown in his marriage.[56] Collins reached a similar conclusion in his essay on John Wesley's relationship with his wife.[57] However, a consideration of the family constellation in which he was raised might shed some light on this phenomenon. These dynamics might also partly explain why, contrary to wisdom, he saw such relationships in an innocent light. His early family constellation is presented in figure 4.2. This constellation formed the primary emotional climate in which he was reared.

As portrayed in the genogram, women largely dominated the early family constellation in which he was nurtured. Although two males were present at his birth, these being his father and his older brother Samuel Jr., they likely exerted little influence in his upbringing during his early formative years.

54. Edwards, *My Dear Sister.*
55. Moore, *Authority.*
56. Collins, *A Real Christian.*
57. Collins, "John Wesley's Relationship."

FIGURE 4.2 The Feminine World of Wesley Prior to Leaving for School
on January 28, 1714

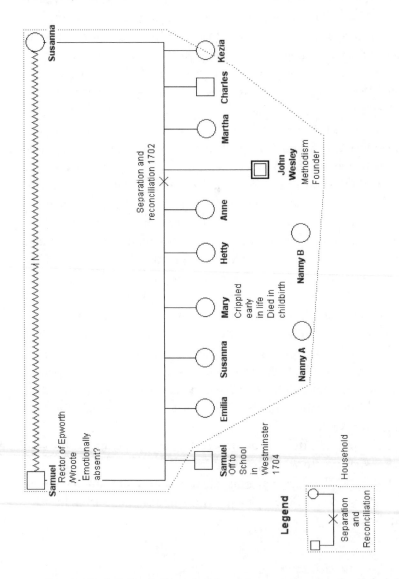

Samuel Jr. left for St. Peter's School in 1704, a year after John's birth.
Additionally, one can characterize his father's presence as one marked
by high boundary ambiguity. Boundary ambiguity is the term used by
Pauline Boss[58] to indicate when one is physically or emotionally unavail-

58. Boss, *Family Stress Mangement.*

able. Although Samuel was physically present to some degree, I would characterize him as emotionally absent, consumed as he was with his parish work and writing his commentaries on the book of Job. For all intent, John's daily world involved the world of females, including his mother Susanna, his sisters, Emilia, Susanna, Mary, Hetty, Anne, and later Martha and two nannies. Rack referred to this reality of John's world as the "feminization of Wesley" and used it to explain his difficult relationships with women during his life. Furthermore, he noted: "The sequel will show that for Wesley both in his spiritual quest and in his relationships with other people, perhaps especially with women; it was above all his mother's influence which would mark his personality and emotional life."[59] This conclusion finds support among other authors. One writer pointed to Susanna's influence on John's imperturbability, whereas he traced Charles' anger and impulsive, emotional style to his father, Samuel.[60]

The influence of his mother and the abundance of females in John's early world likely shaped him in significant ways. No doubt, a preference for the company of women and a familiarity with women was a key part of this influence. We also know his mother's influence extended beyond mere interaction with women. Indeed, the influence of his mother shaped his early views about whether he should marry. As we will discuss in a later chapter, one of Wesley's early mental obstacles to marriage involved the belief in his inability to find a wife like his father had.[61] When one considers this developmental narrative about marriage and openness to it, presented by Heitzenrater, Wesley appears to have moved beyond this early belief. However, I wonder if some residuals of his early beliefs remained. For example, in the same developmental narrative, Wesley eventually arrived at a place where he believed he could marry. But later, one would discover he yet harbored views, which placed marriage at a lower place when compared to ministry. Might he have yet harbored views, which made him compare potential marriage partners to his mother? Significantly, Wesley fell in love with and considered marriage to the three women who nursed him at some point in his life: Sophy Hopkey, Grace Murray, and Mary Vazeille. Given his early belief statements about having a wife like his mother, one might speculate their nursing provided him with concrete examples of their caring nature. In turn, this placed them

59. Rack, *Reasonable Enthusiast*, 60.
60. Edwards, *Sons to Samuel*.
61. Heitzenrater, *Elusive*.

in a favorable light when compared to his mother; their caring actions offered proof he could find someone who was as least as caring and nurtur-
ing as his mother. No wonder he thought of marriage in all three cases.

But, even given this background involving the presence of females,
some evidence suggests John Wesley was not necessarily the best judge of
women. He seemed to approach some of them with some degree of na-
iveté and a trust not often warranted. We find some examples of this early
in his ministry in America. Here I do not refer to Sophy Hopkey, although
some of these traits showed themselves in this relationship. Rather, I refer
to his relationship with Betty Hawkins, the wife of the local doctor. In his
edition of Wesley's journals, Curnock[62] documented Wesley's miscalculation with Mrs. Hawkins. Because of this, he tried to convert her, even
though many signs indicated she possessed no serious interest in religion.
Indeed, rumors placed her in a possible affair with James Oglethorpe,
the leader of the colony. In fact, believing Wesley had started rumors to
this effect, she attacked him on one occasion with pistol and scissors. In
contrast to John's miscalculation, Charles Wesley seemed to have rightly
sized her up. In his journal, he described Mrs. Hawkins as an ungrateful
person, a prostitute, and thorough hypocrite.[63] Other occasions existed
which placed the brothers in disagreement relative to their judgment of
women. In his journal, Charles recorded an occasion where one woman
professed a constant sense of forgiveness and on this basis, John passed
her for the class. Not agreeing with John's judgment, Charles queried her
further and discovered she was still in "the gall of bitterness." The woman
then indicated not only an absence of love but actual hatred for another
sister. Charles noted he would not have believed her justified even if an
angel from heaven testified to it.[64] Admittedly, this latter tale represents
Charles' perspective and might contain some bias. However, these inci-
dents support some difference between John and Charles in their judgment of women, with John appearing less keen in judging their character
and personality. If one admits Charles' possible bias in the latter incident,
the difference seems much clearer in the incident with Mrs. Hawkins.
A more telling case where they apparently differed in judgment about a
female involved none other than the woman whom John married, Mary
Vazeille. But I reserve this discussion for a later chapter.

62. Curnock, "The Journal of the Rev. John Wesley."
63. Wesley, C., *The Journal of the Rev. Charles Wesley,* Vol. 1.
64. Wesley, C., *The Journal of the Rev. Charles Wesley,* Vol. 2.

chapter 5

Multigenerational Transmission Process in the Wesley Family: *Recurring Vocational Themes*

FAMILIES REPEAT THEMSELVES ACROSS generations. Patterns evident in one generation tend to reappear in succeeding generations. For example, if one considers the generations of Abraham, Isaac, and Jacob, one will discover several recurring themes. Favoritism, that is, one parent aligning with one child over against another, shows up repeatedly across the early generations of Abraham's family. Abraham clearly favored Isaac over his older half-brother, Ishmael. The pattern replicated itself in the next generation. Isaac clearly preferred his elder son, Esau, whereas, his wife, Rebekah, favored Jacob (Genesis 25:28). The pattern persisted in the next generation, where Jacob favored Joseph above the rest of his brothers, and celebrated it in giving his son a resplendent coat of many colors. In each generation, favoritism produced rather disastrous results eventuating in sibling rivalry and the consideration of murder of a chosen child. Within these generations, one also finds a consistent pattern where a younger sibling was chosen above an older sibling: Isaac above Ishmael, Jacob above Esau, and Joseph above his brothers. Even in Joseph's family, the younger Ephraim was chosen above the elder Manasseh.

This repetition of family patterns across generations supports Murray Bowen's concept of *Multigenerational Transmission Process.*[1] This concept derives from the systemic nature of families. That is, families relate interdependently. Ties such as their emotional history, biology, culture, and the like, link them together. As a result, changes in any one part tend to reverberate in other parts.[2] But this systemic influence applies not only to

1. Bowen, *Family Therapy.*

2. McGoldrick and Gerson, *Genograms in Family Assessment*; McGoldrick, et al., *Genograms.*

73

families in one generation, it also applies across generations, so that elements in one generation tend to impact other generations. McGoldrick and colleagues captured this essential aspect of families when they indicated the repetition, which occurs in families across succeeding generations. From their perspective ". . . relationship patterns in previous generations may provide implicit models for family functioning in the next generation."[3]

This characteristic appears to apply to the Wesley family. A close observation of the family demonstrates the replication of certain patterns across the generations. In a later chapter, I shall discuss how relational patterns repeated themselves in the Wesley family. However, in the present chapter, I shall focus on recurring vocational patterns in the Wesley family. I shall investigate the predominance of certain careers in the family. In a sense these careers, or vocations, constituted part of the Wesley family business. In this sense, they look a lot like the Kennedy and Bush families of modern America, where involvement in politics appears to comprise part of their DNA. Although the impact of families in this area appears surprising, it shouldn't be. Families influence their members in powerful ways and this influence pervades almost every area including the vocations one chooses. As a result, the following statement carries the ring of truth: ". . . family of origin is a primary variable in the development of attitudes toward ourselves and the way that we perceive ourselves fitting into the world, including the occupational structure."[4]

Vocational Patterns in the Wesley Family

Love of Learning, Music and the Church and her Mission

In *Sons to Samuel*, Edwards[5] cited several examples of Samuel's influence on his sons. The examples he provided point to the influence of multigenerational transmission. Edwards discussed four critical areas in which Samuel influenced his sons: First, he instilled in them a love of learning. In a similar vein, Clarke[6] pointed to the love of learning for which the entire family was known. Contrary to the cultural norm, this love of learning extended even to the girls in the family. Second, according to Edwards,

3. McGoldrick, et al., *Genograms*, 8.

4. Brown and Brooks, *Career Counseling Techniques*, 127.

5. Edwards, *Sons to Samuel*.

6. Clarke, *Memoirs*.

Samuel imparted to his sons a deep commitment to orthodoxy combined with similar dedication to an evangelical emphasis. Third, he nurtured in them a love for the Anglican Church, including its liturgy, sacraments, and music. Finally, from Edward's perspective, Samuel helped them grasp a vision of the church as a worldwide body, and coupled this with an enthusiasm for its mission.[7]

These four areas cited by Edwards point to several vocational influences. In the love of books and learning, Edwards included an emphasis on Samuel's interest in hymn writing, his love of poetry, and the study of Scripture. In fact, according to his brother-in-law, John Dunton, Samuel was much celebrated for his skill in poetry.[8] Anyone who studies John Wesley and his brother, Charles, knows these were important emphases in their lives. Charles was a quintessential hymn-writer having written several thousand hymns. Although John did not rise to the level of his brother in his hymn-writing prowess, he also wrote hymns. We also saw this capability in their brother Samuel who published *Poems on Several Occasions,* which included hymns and humorous pieces. Samuel even wrote poems in honor of the colony in Georgia founded by James Oglethorpe.[9] The brothers also shared their skill in poetry with their talented sister, the tragic Hetty Wesley.

Charles Wesley at his writing Desk, a painting by Richard Douglas at Asbury Theological Seminary. Used with permission.

7. Edwards, *Sons to Samuel.*

8. Dunton, *Life and Errors.*

9. Pudney, *Wesley and His World.*

Samuel's sons also shared with him a love of Scripture. John showed a particular penchant for biblical scholarship, demonstrating familiarity with biblical languages and interpretation of the biblical text as evidenced in his extant commentaries. We saw the same quality in Samuel Junior who was considered a classicist and patrologist.[10] The love for Scripture also resonated in Charles, finding voice in the strong scriptural tenor of his hymns.[11] Along with the writing of poetry and hymns, one can also point to the love of church music and music in general. This vocational transmission showed itself prominently in Charles, who passed down to his sons a love of music and proficiency in its creation. In fact, both sons, Charles Junior and Samuel Wesley, became organists and composers. In the next generation, Charles' grandson, Samuel Sebastian Wesley, became one of the foremost British composers of the nineteenth century.

But as noted, Samuel strongly influenced his sons in their love for the Anglican Church. All three took holy orders and followed their father into the Anglican clergy as high churchmen.[12] Perhaps this love for the church made it difficult for John Wesley to break from the Anglican Church and her practices even after it became clear the Methodist movement was heading in this direction. In this regard, one author described John Wesley as somewhat ecclesiastically schizophrenic, because of his difficulty leaving the Anglican Church even while his preaching and actions sowed the seeds of Methodism's separation from the mother church.[13] On the other hand, John's brother Samuel remained staunch in his commitment to their Anglican roots and showed great distress relative to the direction his brothers were taking. For example, in a letter written to John on April 16, 1739, Samuel warned about the hysteria among the Methodists and the apparent movement towards a split with the Anglicans. He warned John about this and asked him to banish unseemly practices such as extemporaneous expositions and prayers.[14] Samuel betrayed greater distress in his mother, Susanna's, persuasion to the brothers' evangelical teachings. Samuel shared his concerns with his mother in a letter written in October 1739:

10. Baker, *Wesley and the Church of England*.

11. Edwards, *Sons to Samuel*.

12. Baker, *Wesley and the Church of England*; Pudney, *Wesley and His World*.

13. Edwards, *Sons to Samuel*.

14. Welsey, S. J., "Letter to John Wesley," 16 April 1739.

> It was with exceeding concern and grief I heard you had counte-
> nanced a spreading delusion so far as to be one of Jack's congrega-
> tion. Is it not enough that I am bereft of both my brothers, but
> must my mother follow too? I earnestly beseech the Almighty to
> preserve you from joining a schism at the close of your life.... they
> boast of you already as a disciple.[15]

Later as the movement progressed, Charles expressed alarm concerning the perceived movement away from the Anglican Church. For
example, On March 6, 1744, Charles wrote to John about an address the
latter had directed to the King of England. John had written this address
on March 5, 1744, although he later decided to set it aside. The address
titled, *The humble Address of the Societies in England and Wales in deri-
sion called Methodists,* was intended to address two issues. John Wesley
defined these issues in the following language:

> The One, that in spite of all our remonstrances on that head, we
> are continually represented as a peculiar sect of men, separating
> ourselves from the Established Church; The other, that we are still
> traduced as inclined to Popery, and consequently disaffected to
> your Majesty.[16]

In response to this address, Charles wrote, "My objections to your
address in the name of the Methodists is, that it would constitute us a
sect; at least it would *seem to allow* that we are a body distinct from the
national Church; whereas we are only a sound part of that church. Guard
against this; and in the name of the Lord address tomorrow."[17] Given John's
struggles and Charles stance, their final place of burial seems most fitting:
John lays buried outside of the Anglican Church at City Road Chapel,
London, whereas Charles, his wife and a few of his children are firmly
ensconced in an Anglican graveyard at Marylebone.

But Samuel also influenced John and Charles in missionary enthusiasm and interest. In his thirties, Samuel had shown interest in doing
missionary service in India, China, or Abyssinia. He had even proposed
a plan for such work to the Society for the Propagation of the Gospel.[18]
Furthermore, he had shown interest in James Oglethorpe's work in

---

15. Edwards, *Astonishing Youth*, 37.

16. Telford, *The Letters*, Vol. 2, 18.

17. Wesley, *The Journal*, Vol. 1, 354–55.

18. Clarke, *Memoirs*; Edwards, *Family Circle*.

America and had corresponded with the latter about the missionary needs of the young colony.[19] In fact, as indicated earlier, in 1734 he had written to Oglethorpe confessing ". . . a dear love of your colony that if it had been but ten years ago, I would gladly have devoted the remainder of my life and labours to that place . . . "[20] Since he could not go, he suggested to Oglethorpe the names of possible participants.[21] Samuel even tried to persuade Oglethorpe to take his son-in-law, John Whitelamb, husband to his daughter.[22]

Following Bowen's multigenerational transmission concept, it should not surprise the reader to learn these interests in the Wesley brothers even harkened back to earlier generations. Some of these vocational influences are portrayed in Figure 5.1. For example, from the genogram one detects the missionary interests and enthusiasm further back than their father, Samuel. In fact, this interest shows itself in their grandfather John Wesley, who also expressed interest in doing missionary work in the Americas and India.[23] Perhaps, extended family members might also have fostered the interest in foreign lands. For example, we know the Wesleys' uncle, Samuel Annesley, to whose fortune John sometimes referred, had pursued business interests in India.[24] Moreover, John Dunton, Samuel Sr.'s brother-in-law and earlier publishing partner, pursued publishing interests in America and visited it.[25] Surely these influences might have contributed to their larger vision of the world.

19. Pudney, *Wesley and His World.*

20. Edwards, *Family Circle,* 29.

21. Pudney, *Wesley and His World.*

22. Edwards, *Family Circle.*

23. Clarke, *Memoirs.*

24. Clarke, *Memoirs;* Stevenson, *Memorials.*

25. Dunton, *Life and Errors.*

FIGURE 5.1 Careers Interests in the Wesley and Annesley Families[26]

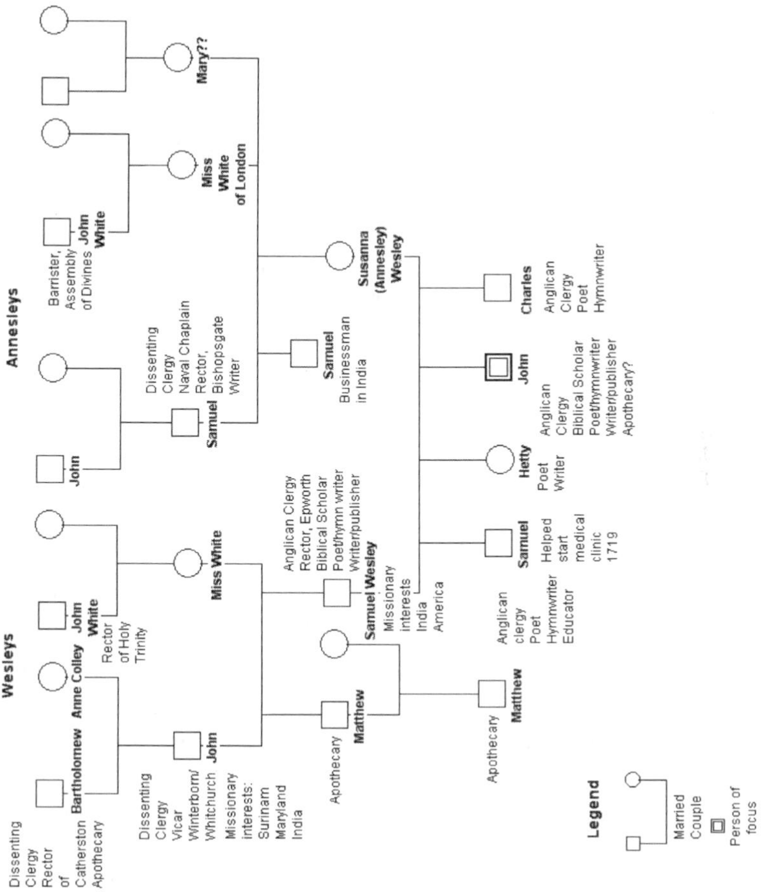

The Dominance of Clergy

The genogram also demonstrates the long line of clergy from which the Wesley's sprung. Clerical careers served as the family business. This vocational reality existed on both sides of the family. For example, Bartholomew Wesley, the great-grandfather of John and Charles Wesley had served as a clergyman, but was thrown out of his living in Charmouth in 1662 through the Act of Uniformity. However, he continued his preaching, supplemented by practicing as an apothecary. Like Bartholomew

26. Based on a variety of sources including Clarke, *Memoirs,* and Rogal, *Susanna Annesley Wesley.*

Wesley, his son, John Wesley of Winterborn/Whitchurch in Dorsetshire, also preached and pastored, but was ejected from his living in 1662. The picture looks remarkably the same on the Annesley side of the family. Here, too, one finds the prominent presence of clergy, including Samuel Annesley, Susanna's father. The Act of Uniformity also caused his ejection from his vicarage at St. Giles in 1662. But, even when one considers females in the Wesley family tree, clergy persons yet predominate. For example, John Wesley of Winterborn/Whitchurch, John's grandfather, married the daughter of Rev. John White, who was a famed puritan and was known as the patriarch of Dorchester. He also served as a member of the committee, which produced the Westminster Confession.[27]

An Interest in Medical Treatment

A perusal of the genogram also shows the transmission of other careers such as biblical writer and publishing. However, it also provides support for another vocation for which John Wesley was known: his interest in treating persons with physical and related ailments. Abelove[28] noted John Wesley's habit of doctoring without charge, treating somatic complaints, and "nervous diseases." Abelove likewise noted Wesley's use of electricity in his treatment of himself and others. In fact, according to him, Wesley placed his electricity apparatus in each of his societies. A. Wesley Hill also gave attention to this interest of Wesley's in his book, *John Wesley Among the Physicians*.[29] Hill noted the many dispensaries, which Wesley opened in cities like London, Bristol, and Newcastle, and his diagnosis and treatment of many patients. Hill offered several reasons for this medical interest in Wesley. First, he noted Wesley's interest in everything pertaining to the good of people, including their physical wellbeing. Second, Wesley saw the tremendous physical needs among the people, and at the time, the number of medical practitioners was inadequate to meet the health needs of the populace. Third, even when available and offered, actual treatment sometimes proved disastrous, utilizing somewhat superficial medical knowledge. Hospital were often appalling places for patients.[30] These reasons provide a good foundation for Wesley's interest in medical

27. Dallimore, *Susanna*.
28. Abelove, *Evangelist of Desire*.
29. Hill, *Wesley Among the Physicians*.
30. Ibid.

practice and the offering of these services. To further this cause, in 1737 Wesley wrote a book on homeopathic medicine called *Primitive Psychic.* Wesley apparently developed his interest in medicine relatively early through reading authors such as Dr. Cheyne's *Book of Health and Long Life.* Wesley also adopted this doctor's prescription for eating, including his recommendation of drinking milk and a vegetable diet.[31]

However, a review of the genogram suggests other possible influences for his interest in medicine. The genogram shows the prominent role of apothecaries in the Wesley family. His great grandfather, Bartholomew Wesley, had studied physic and was often consulted as a physician at Dorsetshire. When he was evicted from his rectorship through the Act of Uniformity, Bartholomew practiced this profession. Apparently, in his day, the terms surgeon, apothecary, and medical practitioner were used interchangeably with physician or doctor.[32] But the tread does not end there. John Wesley's Uncle, Matthew Wesley (who kept close contact with the family), practiced as an apothecary, as did the latter's son.[33] Although not captured in the genogram, we also know his brother-in-law, Richard Harper, the husband of Emilia, practiced as an apothecary. John, himself, had united them in marriage prior to leaving England for Georgia.[34] Besides the presence of these practitioners, his older brother, Samuel, reputedly demonstrated some early interest in medical issues. He apparently contributed to the founding of a clinic in 1719. In writing on the death of Samuel Wesley Jr., one friend wrote, "It is not a little to Mr. Wesley's honor that he was one of the projectors, and a careful and active promoter of the first infirmary set up at Westminster, for the relief of the sick and needy, in the year 1719; and he had the satisfaction to see it greatly flourish from a very small beginning, and to propagate by its example, under the prudent management of other good persons, many pious establishments of the same kind in distant parts of the nation."[35] Stevenson[36] confirmed the founding of this clinic at Westminster and its transition to St. George's Hospital in 1919.

31. Tyerman, *Life and Times.*

32. Clarke, *Memoirs*; Stevenson, *Memorials.*

33. Clarke, *Memoirs.*

34. Maser, *Story of John Wesley's Sisters.*

35. Clarke, *Memoirs*, 443.

36. Stevenson, *Memorials.*

Medical Interests and the Role of Physical Illness in the Wesley Family

Following Bowen's concept of multigenerational transmission process, I suspect these vocational influences in the family helped shape Wesley. Moreover, I suspect other dynamics, including factors within the family, might have served to develop an early interest in medicine in John Wesley. One contributing influence likely stemmed from the presence of continual illness in the family. Reading Arnold Dallimore's book on Susanna, I was struck by an early comment Samuel Wesley made about his wife. Samuel wrote the comment around the time of the birth of their third child Emilia, ". . . my wife's lying about last Christmas and threatening to do the same the next, and 2 children and as many servants to provide for (my wife being sickly, having had 3 or 4 touches of her rheumatism again, though we always fight it away with whey."[37] The comment indicated Susanna's frequent ailments such as rheumatism. Judging from the statement, one might plausibly assume the connection of her frequent illnesses to her equally frequent pregnancies. But I make the connection to family illness for an additional reason. During my examination of the Wesley family papers in March 2008 at John Rylands Library, the many references to family illness in the letters surprised me. Among the illnesses, I would include mental problems such as depression. Although one could explain frequent illness due to the physical conditions of Wesley's day, the prevalence of illness in the family yet took me by surprise. One early reference to illness appeared in a letter quoted earlier and written by Susanna to her son, Samuel, on October 11, 1709. In the letter she described her recovery from deep depression, which had started after the fire of February 9, 1709 and had persisted since then. Susanna wrote:

> Tho nothing in the world could ever make me forget you or prevent my having the tenderest regard for ye happiness, and concern for ye immortal soul; yet my mind has bin so terribly shock'ed by our late misfortunes, that tho I cannot say I never had leisure, yet I couldn't dispose myself to write to ye. A long series of adverse fortunes had before inclin'd me to a too melancholy temper, but this most strange and surprising accident attended by too many calamitous circumstances gave my soul so strong a bent to extreme sadness that I haven't bin able to recover myself (till not

---

37. Dallimore, *Susanna,* 35.

a few days?); but have bin as one dead to ye world, uncapable of enjoying any of those comforts . . . [38]

But Susanna suffered other difficulties besides this prolonged bout with depression. The content of several letters showed many bouts of physical illness. For example, in a letter to her brother, Samuel Annesley, written on January 20, 1721, Susanna wrote, "What we shall or shall not need hereafter God only knows, but at present there hardly ever was a greater coincidence of unprosperous events in one family than is now ours. *I am rarely in health, Mr. Wesley declines apace . . .* "[39] (Italics mine). The letter looms important for several reasons, including an attempt by Susanna to settle a financial dispute between her husband and her brother. But for our purposes, the section from the letter highlighted above demonstrates the calamitous events in the family and her precarious health as well as the declining state of her husband. Besides this example, other material highlighted the state of her ill health. In fact, one bout of illness proved severe enough for her to contemplate an impending death. This instance occurred in July 1727. In a letter written to John and Charles Wesley by their father on July 5, 1727, Samuel expressed concerns about Suzanna's health.[40] Although I am at pains to explain it, on the reverse of this said letter, Susanna wrote John a letter in which she mentioned her recovery from ill health. The two letters disagree on whether she was yet ill or had recovered. Yet, they confirm her illness. The circumstances of her health provoked John to write his father with condolences about his mother's approaching demise. Samuel responded to this correspondence from John on July 18, 1727, and though Susanna did not die, he noted ". . . Susanna has grown thin from sick fits . . . "[41]

Around 1731 we find yet another reference to illness in Susanna. On this occasion, her sister, Anne Annesley, who apparently had heard of Susanna's illness, wrote to her on August 12, 1731, "I hope to hear better news when my nephews return to London for they told me you had a very ill state of health."[42] The year 1732 seemed to have brought another period of illness for Susanna. In a letter written to John on February 21,

38. Welsey, Susanna, "Letter from Epworth," October 11, 1709.

39. Wesley, Susanna, "Letter from Epworth to her brother Samuel Annesley."

40. Wesley, Samuel, "Letter from Wroot," 5 Jul 1727.

41. Wesley, Samuel, "Letter from Wroot."

42. Annesley, "Letter from Anne Annesley," 12 August, 1731.

1732, Susanna wrote, "I thank God I am much better than I have bin (sic), tho far from being in health, yet a little respite from much pain, I esteem a great mercy."[43] In the same letter, Susanna continued:

> I have time enough now, more than I can make a good life of, but yet for many reasons, I care not to write to anyone. I never did much good in my life when in the best of health and vigour, and therefore think it not be presumption in me to hope to be useful now; 'tis more than I can wel (sic) do to bear my own infirmity and other sufferings as I ought and would do.

This letter appears to confirm a period of continued illness for Susanna. Moreover, in October of the same year, she wrote to John indicating she would have written sooner ". . . had I not been at liberty from pain of body, and other severer trials not convenient to mention."[44]

But as implied by Susanna's letter of January 20, 1721, Samuel, her husband also appears to have suffered prolonged ill health. A letter from their son, Samuel written on May 11, 1719 implied Samuel Senior's illness. Samuel wrote:

> Honoured Sir,
>
> My mother tells me that you want to know how accounts stand between you and I, and that you were indisposed so as not well to be able to write; I am exceeding sorry for the ill news . . . [45]

Samuel's words might simply point to some debilitating illness, which disinclined his father to write. However, in reading some of the family letters written by Samuel Wesley Senior, I noticed what appears to be significant deterioration in his writing. An early letter written on May 18, 1701 to Archbishop John Sharpe showed a strong hand.[46] However, a letter written to John and Charles on June 21, 1727 showed majors problems suggesting some physical decline in his ability to write. This letter proved very difficult to read because the letters appeared ill formed as well as less tightly put together. They also looked much larger and less legible than earlier letters.[47] These characteristics suggest a person who was

43. Wesley, Susanna, "Letter to John Wesley," 21 Feb, 1732.

44. Wesley, Susanna, "Photographic copy of a letter," 25 Oct, 1732.

45. Wesley, S. J., "Letter to his father," 11 May 1719.

46. Wesley, Samuel, "Letter to Archbishop John Sharpe," May 18, 1701.

47. Wesley, Samuel, "Letter from Wroot," 21 June 1727.

experiencing major difficulties forming letters. The shaky writing seems like something one would expect of a person suffering from decreased dexterity and less control of muscles and movement necessary for writing. The poor quality of the writing possibly indicates some Parkinson's related disorder. Surprisingly, in another letter from Samuel, written on July 18, 1727,[48] Samuel Wesley reverts to a much tighter pattern suggesting the earlier letter of 1701. However, the writing appeared different. One can reasonably conclude Samuel did not write this letter of July 18, but dictated it to someone else who did the actual writing. The signature at the end of the letter supports this conclusion in that it conformed to the deteriorated quality of writing seen in the June 1727 letter.[49] The deteriorated signature appears the same in one of Samuel's letter from January 21, 1735.[50] This evidence leads one to wonder whether during 1727, or perhaps even as early as Samuel Jr.'s letter of May 1719, Samuel Senior had experienced some illness, which compromised his physical ability to write legibly. This compromise in his physical capabilities, at least related to writing, appears to have extended down through 1735, the year of his death.

Other evidence from the letters confirms Samuel's illness during 1727. For example, in the June 1727 letter, Samuel mentioned, ". . . creeping out of my cave this midsummer," a likely reference to being confined to his home because of illness.[51] Moreover, in the letter written in July 5, 1727, Samuel first raised the issue to John and Charles of succeeding him at Wroote.[52] This concern might have arisen from some of his physical problems, and a fear of his imminent demise. One finds yet more specific references to his illness and impending death in 1732. The evidence comes from a letter written by Susanna on October 25, 1732, referenced earlier. Susanna wrote in a postscript:

> Ye Father is in a very bad state of health, he sleeps little, and eats less. He seems not to have any apprehension of his approaching exit; but I fear that he has but a short time to live. 'Tis with much pain and difficulty, that he performs Divine service on the Lord's Day, which sometimes he is forced to contract very much. Everybody observes his decay but himself, and people really seem

48. Wesley, Samuel, "Letter from Wroot," July 18, 1727.

49. Wesley, Samuel, "Letter from Wroot," 21 June 1727.

50. Wesley, Samuel, "Letter from Epworth," 21 January, 1935.

51. Wesley, Samuel, "Letter from Wroot," 21 June 1727.

52. Wesley, Samuel, "Letter from Wroot," 5 Jul 1727.

much concerned both for him and his family. The two girls, being uneasy in the present situation, do not apprehend the bad consequences which (in all appearance) must attend his death so much or I think they ought to do; for as bad as they think their condition now, I doubt it will be far worse when his head is laid.[53]

A final piece of evidence for Samuel's illness comes from his letter to John on January 21, 1735. Samuel appears to have dictated this letter as he had the letter of July 18, 1727. One concludes this from the highly legible writing as well as its flair and ease of reading. As indicated earlier, the signature looks different than the body of the letter, conforming to his sick letter of June 1727. In this letter, Samuel ponders his death and fears he would die leaving his commentary incomplete. By now he felt so weak, he could not leave his bedchamber.[54] He would die within a few short months of this letter, expiring on April 25, 1735.[55] The astute reader might have noted some coincidence in the illnesses of Susanna and Samuel: they both experienced significant illnesses during the years 1727 and 1732. What a difficult time this must have been for the family. Given the evidence, I suspect both Samuel and Susanna Wesley suffered from chronic illnesses for many years prior to their deaths.

Other Wesley family letters exhibit the recurring theme of illness in its members, however, for the sake of space I will point to two other persons: The first example comes from Anne Wesley Lambert, the sibling born before John and the twin sister of his brother, John Benjamin. Speaking about her, Frederick Maser concluded she was one of the few Wesley women who found happiness and whose life proceeded as a quiet stream.[56] I disagree with his conclusion in some respects; in the Wesley family letters, I found evidence suggesting Anne and her son Jacky Lambert lived in deplorable poverty for some time.[57] Perhaps her poverty and deprivation compromised her health. At any rate, in a letter written by Emilia to John on March 14, 1730, she wrote, "Poor Sister Lambert has such ill health that I fear she will not live long."[58] Unfortunately, though

---

53. Wesley, Susanna, "Photographic copy of a letter," 25 Oct, 1732.

54. Welsey, Samuel, "Letter from Epworth," 21 January, 1935.

55. Clarke, *Memoirs*.

56. Maser, *Story of John Wesley's Sisters*.

57. Wesley, S. J., "Letter to Susanna Wesley," 3 July 1731; "Letter from Salisbury," April 29, 1736.

58. Wesley, E., "Letter to John Wesley," February 9, 1730.

she did not die that year, we do not know when she died. She mysteriously dropped from the pages of her family history. We do know she appeared at her mother's death in 1742. After that event, she apparently disappeared from the face of the earth, with no known account of the rest of her life and when and where she died. Some think she died shortly after her mother's death.[59] Kezia, the youngest Wesley sibling also experienced major bouts with illness. Maser[60] confirmed her experience with illness most of her life, dying at the youthful age of thirty-two. In the same letter in which Emilia mentioned Anne Lambert's ill health, she also highlighted kezia's chronic illness. "Poor Kez is almost confounded between the fevor (sic) on one hand and the green sickness on the other. She is always taking some hops, and yet can't keep well."[61]

Various family members wrote the letters to John Wesley highlighted in this section. How could they fail to influence him? They likely influenced him in a similar manner, as often occurs in the lives of physicians. The prototypical story for persons entering medical fields is one of growing up in a family where chronic illness existed. Such persons usually felt helpless in the face of the family's illness. Thus, a medical career became a way to vicariously rescue the family they could not save in actuality. A similar story exists in the career journeys of those who enter psychological and counseling fields. In some instances, mental illness existed in the home during the individual's formative years. In this case, entering the mental health field partly represents an effort to vicariously save their loved one by their career. In other cases, perhaps the individual had sought counseling at some critical juncture in life. In this sense, entering a mental health field involves the return of a favor; doing for others what had been done for them.[62] Growing up with illness of various sorts seems to influence the career choice of physicians, counselors, and other health care professionals. His experiences with illness likely influenced John Wesley in a similar manner.

59. Maser, *Story of John Wesley's Sisters.*

60. Ibid.

61. Wesley, E., "Letter to John Wesley," February 9, 1730.

62. Corey and Corey, *Becoming a Helper.*

chapter 6

Relational Patterns in
the Wesley Family

B ESIDES VOCATIONAL PATTERNS, OTHER relational family patterns also
recur across generations. These two patterns relate to each other. This
ought not to surprise. Since family involves a system; its parts as well as
its patterns interconnect. Relationship ties and patterns often exert significant influence on vocational direction. This truth existed in the Wesley
family. Across the two generations of the Epworth household there existed
a tendency for members to dictate to other members their vocational direction. Some evidence suggests Samuel directly influenced John to enter holy orders. In his own words, John Wesley stated as much when he
wrote, "When I was about twenty-two, my father pressed me to enter into
holy orders."[1] Despite this personal testimony from John in 1738, Frank
Baker, the eminent Wesley historian, insisted the initiative to enter holy
orders came from John and not his father. However, Baker acknowledged
Samuel's encouragement of his son's desire. In so doing, John would be
joining the fourth generation of clergy in the family.[2] Charles Wesley's
entry into Holy Orders seems a much more definitive example of the
tendency for family to influence vocational direction. Speaking to his
own entry into Holy Orders, Charles indicated: "I took my degree; and
only thought of spending my days in Oxford: But my brother who always
had the ascendency over me, persuaded me to accompany him and Mr.
Oglethorpe to Georgia. I exceedingly dreaded entering into Holy Orders;
but he overruled me here also . . ."[3] John's ability to influence Charles in
these matters suggests some possible problems of self-differentiation in
the latter. Indeed, a statement made by John Gambold, a member of the

1. Curnock, "The Journal," Vol. 1, 13; Ward and Heitzenrater, *The Works*, Vol. 18, 120.

2. Baker, "Investigating."

3. Edwards, *Sons to Samuel*, 36; Lloyd, *Charles Wesley*, 46.

Holy Club, seems to confirm this. Gambold noted, "I never observed any person have a more real deference for another, than [Charles] had for his brother. . . . He followed his brother entirely. Could I describe one of them, I should describe both."[4]

John Wesley in his late twenties or early thirties. A painting by Richard Douglas at Asbury Theological Seminary. Used with permission.

But John's interference into Charles' vocational life seemed but a small part of a larger pattern in the Wesley family. Interference into each other's life characterized the Wesley clan. Frederick Maser suggested as much when he noted:

> The Wesleys were a close-knit family but they were not always in harmony. They interfered with one another's lives and loves and often wrought havoc by their actions. Nevertheless, each manifested his or her own independence and managed to survive the most dismal circumstances. In general, the Wesleys were survivors.[5]

Maser's comment about the family speaks to several recurring patterns in the Wesley family. What Maser referred to as closeness could

4. Lloyd, *Charles Wesley*, 44.

5. Maser, *Story of John Wesley's Sisters*, 3–4.

better be termed "enmeshment." That is, the family exhibited a suffocating closeness, which hindered individual members from making their own decisions and pursuing their own paths. The interference of which Maser spoke likely resulted from this closeness. However, members in the family would likely think their closeness gave them the duty and right to interfere in each other's lives, and even to make decisions for each other. Yet, each individual in such a situation maintains an innate need to think and decide his or her own course. This need likely contributed on occasion to a striving for independence by Wesley family members, creating perceived rebellion and causing disharmony in the family. Perhaps this is what Maser meant when he spoke of the "independence" exhibited in the midst of family interference.

In this chapter, I shall discuss three major relational patterns, which existed in the Wesley family. Specifically, I shall address the pattern of individuation and enmeshment, the tendency to emotionally cut off and distance, and the pattern of interference. In my opinion, these patterns merit some discussion because they provide clues into the relational patterns evident in John Wesley's life and ministry.

Individuation and Enmeshment in the Wesley Family

In chapter 1, I discussed the nature of individuation. There I suggested it entailed the ability to differentiate from one's family of origin on the journey to becoming a healthy and mature individual.[6] Differentiation also involves a process whereby one moves from early family attachments, especially to mothers, and becomes emotionally autonomous in relation to family and others.[7] Differentiation includes two dimensions: First, it includes an intrapsychic dimension allowing differentiation between feelings and thinking so as not to confuse emotional reasoning with objective thinking. Second, it comprises an interpersonal dimension, which allows individuals to maintain a distinct sense of self even in emotional relationships with others. This dimension permits intimacy with others while maintaining one's autonomy.[8]

6. Blessing, "Murray Bowen's"; Bowen, *Family Therapy*; Nichols, *Family Therapy*; Skowron, "Differentiation of Self"; Titelman, "Emotional Cutoff."

7. Titelman, "Emotional Cutoff."

8. Bowen, *Family Therapy*; Nichols, *Family Therapy*; Nichols and Schwartz, *Family Therapy*; Skowron, "Differentiation of Self."

What are the consequences when individuals do not differentiate themselves from their family of origin? Many consequences ensue, though I will only highlight two. First, a lack of differentiation often exhibits itself in dependency. Persons fail to develop appropriate independence (or interdependence) and instead become overly dependent on family of origin members. Second, lack of differentiation eventuates in interpersonal enmeshment or described another way, fusion with others.[9] Indeed, enmeshment forms the logical other side of individuation. Given the concomitant confusion of feeling with thinking, the fused individual might think enmeshment is appropriate and even healthy. This poses all kinds of problems for the formation of intimate relationships. Persons enmeshed with their families of origin find it almost impossible to truly leave their families to give themselves to intimate relationships. Appropriately, family experts see the resolution of emotional attachment to family as a necessary first step for marriage readiness.[10]

A somewhat exaggerated (though real) example might demonstrate the problems with this latter aspect of enmeshment. Although I am not in the habit of reading *Dear Abby,* while perusing the local newspaper, the headline, *Wife of 5 Years Hasn't Moved in Yet,* caught my attention. In the column, a rather distraught husband wrote to ask Dear Abby's advice on how to deal with his wife. He was married to his 40 years old wife for five years. However, she still had not moved into his home. In fact, she had not even relocated her personal belongings. According to the husband's complaint, his wife ran to her mother's house six days a week. When he raises this issue with her, she promises to move her stuff to their home but never does. Dear Abby rightly diagnosed the problem, stating this wife was having "an unusually hard time severing the umbilical cord."[11] This constitutes a clear case of enmeshment with her mother, making it impossible for her to truly and fully become a wife and bond with her husband. Enmeshment creates all kinds of problems of this sort.

But how does this pattern apply to the Wesley family? First, the Wesleys appeared to exhibit some traits of enmeshment and dependency. John's ability to influence Charles' vocational direction, and indeed his journey to America, seems to indicate some enmeshment or lack of indi-

9. Bowen, *Practice of Psychotherapy*; Nichols, *Family Therapy*; Nichols and Schwartz, *Family Therapy*.

10. Carter and McGoldrick, *Family Life Cycle*.

11. Van Buren, "Wife of 5 Years."

viduation and some dependency. Beyond this, dependency on Susanna by her children might have been a characteristic of the family. V. H. H. Green and others have reached this conclusion, suggesting Susanna's dominance in the home led to a dependency on her in all her children.[12] However, in this section, I will illustrate the difficulties family members' experienced in forming new intimate relationships and readjusting family of origin connections. In so doing, I hope to demonstrate the enmeshment and corresponding problems in individuation, which characterized many persons in the Wesley family.

John and Charles' Misgivings in Intimate Relationships

Several Wesley children experienced difficulties in these areas. However, for this discussion I shall focus on the difficulties exhibited by John and Charles in forming intimate relationships and readjusting their relationship to each other. At the outset, it seems important to observe the relative lateness in coming to marriage exhibited by both men: Charles married around age 40 and John tied the knot when he was almost 48. This delay might have derived from their commitment to the Methodist revival and the demands it placed on them. John stated as much, fearing marriage might become an impediment to the gospel, "But my grand objection to these twelve years past has been, 'A dispensation of the Gospel has been committed to me. And I will do nothing which directly or indirectly tends to hinder my preaching of the Gospel'"[13] Correspondingly, when he decided to marry, he did so because he thought it would further his ministry. But, in the same document where these words occur, John provided a developmental account of his journey from believing he should not marry to believing marriage to Grace Murray was appropriate. Among these reasons, John mentioned the inability to find a wife like his mother, his inability to keep a wife, his belief that it was unlawful for priests to marry, and the expense marriage would incur.[14]

But even after such considerations, John vacillated in his relationships. Charles also seemed to struggle, but appeared to do so to a lesser degree. Nevertheless, even after Charles proposed to Sarah Gwynne on April 3, 1748, he experienced second thoughts. Following his proposal on

12. Green, *Young Mr. Wesley*; Moore, *Authority*.

13. Heitzenrater, *Elusive*, 181.

14. Ibid.

April 4, 1748, Charles recorded in shorthand in his journal his fear result-ing from his commitment; he second-guessed himself for making it, and chided his rashness in revealing his intentions.[15] One might reasonably attribute his second thoughts to anxiety generated in a man who had re-mained single for many years. However, his second-guessing and regrets might also betray some innate fear of committing to an intimate relation-ship. On the other hand, John's vacillations in relationships appear far more legendary and much more definitive. Several authors have pointed to the extreme wavering demonstrated in John Wesley's relationships with Sophy Hopkey and Grace Murray.[16] John's vacillation clearly appears in his relationship with Sophy Hopkey in Georgia. Speaking about this relationship, one author offered:

> Here, even if there was no formal declaration, there can hardly be any doubt that Wesley was in love and would have liked to marry Sophy, but was torn by conflicts between love, duty, notions of the value of celibacy and more obscure difficulties in his own nature which led him to blow alternately hot and cold until the bewil-dered girl married elsewhere.[17]

In a similar vein, another author described Wesley's relationship with Hopkey as involving a quasi-engagement complicated by John's struggle to find freedom and a clear path of duty.[18] On February 3, 1737, John wrote in his diary:

> I was now in a great strait. I still thought it best for me to live single. And this was still my design; but I felt the foundations of it shaken more and more every day. Insomuch that I again hinted at a desire of marriage, though I made no direct proposal. For indeed it was only a sudden thought which had not the consent of my own mind.[19]

The words in this entry betray a man caught between reason and conflict-ing emotions. Reason beckoned him to remain single, but his emotions—strongly clinging to his love interest—furtively snuck out in a kind of lexical leakage veiled in hints and indirect proposals of marriage, which

15. Wesley, C., *The Journal*, Vol. 2.

16. Collins, *A Real Christian*; Curnock, "The Journal"; Dobree, *Biography*; Rack, *Reasonable Enthusiast*; Ward and Heitzenrater, *The Works*, Vol. 18.

17. Rack, *Reasonable Enthusiast*, 258.

18. Curnock, "The Journal."

19. Curnock, "The Journal," Vol. 1, 315.

were then quickly regretted. In many ways, John's words remind me of Charles' immediate regrets after proposing marriage to Sarah. However, Charles' mental resolve did not intervene quickly enough to block the direct proposal as did John's. John continued his vacillation even after he decided, through the casting of lots, not to consider the matter further. In fact, on March 7, when he again met Sophy, but for the interruption of Mr. Causton (Sophy's uncle), he would have broken his resolve. Betraying the conflict between his reason and emotions, he then thought this a narrow escape in which he had once more been "snatched as a brand out of the fire."[20] On March 9, 1737, William Williamson secured the Caustons' approval to marry their niece, Sophy Hopkey, an event, which caused great consternation in Wesley. In fact, he regarded this day a devastatingly sorrowful one in his life and wrote:

> No such day since I first saw the sun! O deal tenderly with thy servant! Let me not see such another![21]

Other sentiments expressed in his diary confirm this assessment. His entries showed a man tormented by emotions and plunged into deep distress and bewilderment. These feelings persisted even when he prayed, or at least tried to pray. All these distressing emotions directly erupted from the upcoming marriage of his beloved Sophy to William Williamson.[22] According to Curnock, Wesley wrote his final account of his experience with Sophy Hopkey on March 12, 1738, while at Oxford. Curnock believed Wesley wrote this account more briefly and hurriedly at an earlier date. He assumed the account represented for Wesley "a psychological review of motives and emotions by a man torn by inward conflict—a conflict between duty and affection."[23] The date of March 12 appears highly significant: Following Curnock's timeline, John Wesley first met Sophy on March 13, 1736, although he acknowledged the date of March 12 as one cited by others. Sophy Hopkey also married William Williamson March 12, 1737. The coincidence in the date of the first meeting, Sophy's marriage, and the writing of the final account suggests an anniversary event. On or around March 12, all the hurtful feelings of that significant loss would come flooding back to Wesley's heart and mind.

20. Ibid.
21. Ibid. 330.
22. Curnock, "The Journal," Vol. 1; Heitzenrater, *Elusive*.
23. Curnock, "The Journal," Vol. 1, 288.

Moreover, during this same period, John thought his brother, Charles, was dying of pleurisy.[24] Most likely, his thoughts about the impending loss of his brother during this emotionally charged period compounded his reawakened pain regarding Miss Sophy. The writing of the account likely provided John a cathartic release of pain long buried, now exacerbated by freshly minted hurt occasioned by the possible loss of his brother, Charles. Besides providing cathartic release, the completion of the account likely provided some degree of closure for John Wesley.

One would think the experience with Sophy Hopkey would have created in John less vacillation in future relationships. But this was not necessarily the case. Similar vacillation appeared in his relationship with Grace Murray several years later. However, with Grace, John displayed greater expressed commitment, contracting legal promises of marriage in July and September of 1749.[25] By this time Wesley had moved beyond his beliefs about celibacy. He now thought Grace Murray would serve as a suitable partner and would not encumber him with additional expense or hinder the gospel.[26] In fact, John concluded Grace the most appropriate mate for him:

15. First as a housekeeper. . . .
16. As a nurse. . . .
17. As a companion. . . .
18. As a friend. . . .
19. Lastly, as a fellow labourer in the Gospel of Christ (the light wherein my wife is to be chiefly considered) . . ."[27]

Wesley's utilitarian reasons for marrying Grace Murray glaringly appear in this quotation. But as I indicate elsewhere, this appears consistent with Wesley's perspective on the connection between ministry and marriage; the latter must always serve the former. But Wesley genuinely loved Grace Murray and desired to marry her in fulfillment of his de praesenti contracts. However, Charles and others within Methodist circles raised objections to the marriage. They thought Grace Murray too low bred for John. Furthermore, they argued, his marriage to her would turn the

24. Curnock, "The Journal," Vol. 1.

25. Baker, "Investigating;" Collins, *A Real Christian*; Curnock, "The Journal"; Dobree, *Biography*; Heitzenrater, *Elusive*; Maser, "Only Marriage; Rack, *Reasonable Enthusiast*.

26. Heitzenrater, *Elusive*.

27. Ibid. 182.

Methodist preachers against John and his authority and generally break up the societies.[28] Unconvinced by these arguments, John purposed to marry her, still deeming Grace the most appropriate person for him to marry.[29]

Believing as he did, one wonders why John did not hasten to formalize marriage to Grace, especially when she pressed him to do so. His hesitation resembles a similar vacillation evident in the Sophy Hopkey affair. As in that relationship, John loved a woman and desired marriage, but found it difficult to take the final plunge. To address Grace's petitions, John argued his need to take three steps before formalizing marriage: make matters right with John Bennet, one of Wesley's preachers and a rival for Grace Murray's hand; obtain Charles' consent; and seek the prayers and understanding of the Methodists preachers and people.[30] Before John could complete these steps and marry Grace, his brother Charles rushed her into a marriage with John Bennet. Although one could lay a large amount of blame at Charles' door, and to a lesser extent, at John Bennet's, one must also fault John Wesley. According to one author, John's oblique proposals and his many reservations and hesitations opened the door wide to John Bennet.[31] Once again, John saw a potential bride plucked right from under his nose.

Following his knowledge of these unfortunate events, John's devastation appeared as acute as it previously did with Sophy Hopkey. Speaking about the aftermath from John's diary, Curnock noted ". . . a searching self-examination quite in the manner of his earlier diaries and Journal, with an acute and elaborate analysis of the effects produced by inordinate affection."[32] In his diary entries, John wrote, " I was in great heaviness, my heart was sinking in me like a stone. Only so long as I was preaching I felt ease. When I had done, the weight returned. I went to Church sorrowful and very heavy, though I knew not any particular cause. And God found me there . . ."[33] Similar sentiments appear in a letter John wrote to Thomas Bigg of Newcastle on October 7, 1749, four days after Grace's marriage to John Bennet:

28. Ibid.

29. Abelove, *Evangelist of Desire*; Heitzenrater, *Elusive*.

30. Baker, "Investigating."

31. Rack, *Reasonable Enthusiast*.

32. Curnock, "The Journal," Vol. 3, 432.

33. Ibid. 435.

Leeds, October 7th, 1749
MY DEAR BROTHER,

Since I was six years old, I never met with such a severe trial as for some days past. For ten years God has been preparing a fellow-labourer for me by a wonderful train of providences. Last year I was convinced of it; therefore I delayed not, but, as I thought, made all sure beyond a danger of disappointment. But we were soon torn asunder by a whirlwind. In a few months, the storm was over; I then used more precaution than before, and fondly told myself, that the day of evil would return no more. But it soon returned. The waves rose again since I came out of London. I fasted and prayed, and strove all I could; but the sons of Zeruiah were too hard for me. The whole world fought against me, but above all my own familiar friend. Then the word was fulfilled, "Son of man, behold, I take from thee the desire of thine eyes at a stroke; yet shalt thou not lament, neither shall thy tears run down."

The fatal irrevocable stroke was struck on Tuesday last. Yesterday I saw my friend (that was), and him to whom she is sacrificed. I believe you never saw such a scene. But "why should a living man complain, a man for the punishment of his sins?"

I am, yours affectionately,
John Wesley[34]

If John had not hesitated in formalizing his marriage to Grace, these events likely would not have unfolded in this fashion. But once again, vacillation, likely bred from hesitancy in establishing intimate relationships, undid his plans. In his psychological study of John Wesley, Robert Moore[35] attributed Wesley's hesitancy in intimate relationships with his early experiences in his home. Specifically, according to him, John learned to guard against carnal passions and human sexuality from his mother, Susanna. Moore saw this teaching as a partial explanation for Wesley's reference to inordinate affection in the aftermath of losing Grace Murray. For Moore, this background created in John a type of approach-avoidance conflict relative to intimate relationships; that is, John would develop attraction to a woman, but given the early script about such relationships, he would experience conflict because of the attraction. In essence, it created for John a conflict between attraction and conscience.[36] Others have

---

34. Telford, *Life of John Wesley,* 249.

35. Moore, *Authority.*

36. Ibid.

drawn similar conclusions. For example, speaking of the Grace Murray affair, one writer noted the parallels between this relationship and that with Sophy Hopkey. Given the similarity in vacillation, the tragic ending, and John's emotional repercussions, the author concluded:

> . . . this was not simply a tragedy of errors but further evidence of some deep-rooted psychological disability in his nature as regards relationships with women.[37]

Besides the possibility of an inner conflict regarding intimate relationships, one could also argue for another potential source of conflict. As I will argue later, the many cases of unhappy marriages in his family of origin might have provided some basis for approaching committed relationships with a jaundiced eye.

John and Charles' Misgivings about Each Other's Intimate Relationships

But John and, to a lesser extent, Charles did not just struggle with their own intimate relationships, the brothers also experienced misgivings about each other's significant relationships and possible marriages. Although other reasons might have caused them to recoil from the other's impending marriage, their deep connection to each other might have played a major role; that is, their connection to each other made for difficult personal adjustments to the other's marriage. Since Charles was the first to marry, I start with John's apparent difficulties with Charles' marriage. Charles first met his future wife, Sarah Gwynne, on August 28, 1747. Similar to the role of illness in the formation of John's relationships, Sarah nursed Charles for nine days during the latter's illness. Charles would propose to her several months later in April, 1748.[38] From Charles' perspective, John experienced difficulty at the prospect of his marriage. In his journal entry for Tuesday April 19, 1748, Charles indicated the communication of his developing intention to his brother, noting no encouragement or objection from John. The communication of his intentions sprung from an earlier pact made between the brothers; namely, neither would seek marriage nor move in that direction without first making the other aware and seeking the other's consent. When Charles made his intentions

37. Rack, *Reasonable Enthusiast*, 257.
38. Lloyd, *Charles Wesley*; Wesley, C., *The Journal.*

known, John actually proposed three names, including Sarah's, and John heartily approved Charles' choice of the latter. He even agreed to provide the necessary financial proofs, which the Gwynne family required to consent to the marriage. However, the following April, when they had made their way to Ireland for the marriage, John balked. Charles, evidently distraught, recorded the event. In his journal entry, he recorded how his brother ". . . appeared full of scruples and refused to go to Garth at all."[39] Charles had to make great effort to hold his temper and commit the circumstances to God. The next day, Charles made a similar entry in his journal. This entry also implied John's reticence at the thought of his brother's marriage. Sunday, April 2nd. ". . . I had wrote our friends notice, that I should be at Cardiff tomorrow, and on Tuesday or Wednesday at Garth. But I found my brother had appointed to preach in several places till Friday; Which I did not take kindly."[40] To his credit, John rose above his misgivings after meeting with Sarah's mother, and cleared the way for the marriage on April 8, 1749.[41] Charles' marriage to Sarah likely prompted a similar desire in John. His tentative decision to marry came within a few months of his brother's decision. Furthermore, in August 1748, with similar indirectness as he had demonstrated with Sophy Hopkey, John made his first tentative proposal of marriage. He said Grace: "If ever I marry, I think you will be the person."[42] The near synchronicity of these events suggests Charles' engagement and marriage likely influenced John's decisions. In his dissertation on Charles Wesley, Lloyd[43] came to this conclusion. He suggested John chose to marry Grace Murray because of the loss of his deepest relationship with Charles. By so doing, he sought to replace Charles' place in his life by Grace Murray. He reached a similar conclusion relative to John's marriage to Mary Vazeille.

But John's proposed marriage to Grace Murray brought a harsh reaction in Charles. As indicated earlier, Charles cast aspersions on Grace's low breeding to deter John. Moreover, he indicated the calamitous results for Methodism if such a marriage was solemnized, but all to

---

39. Wesley, C., *The Journal*, Vol. 2, 54.

40. Ibid.

41. Lloyd, *Charles Wesley*; Wesley, C., *The Journal*.

42. Baker, "Investigating," 177.

43. Lloyd, *Charles Wesley*.

no avail.[44] Eventually, Charles, in a rash and impulsive manner rushed Grace Murray into marriage with John Bennet. Because of these actions, Charles has gained notoriety for disrupting John's real chance at love in the potential marriage to Grace Murray. However, when viewed in light of the interference pattern in the family, his behavior seems less reviling, though devastating in its impact on John. After all, interference in each other's relationships characterized the family and was not only peculiar to Charles. Through interference, the Wesleys sought to protect its vulnerable members. Thus, Charles' behavior might be seen as an attempt to protect John from himself as well as Methodism's viability. But given our previous discussion, this behavior also sprung from the heightened enmeshment and lack of differentiation in the Wesley family. Because of the lack of differentiation, Charles experienced negative emotions from the thoughts of losing his brother, John. Indeed, according to one author, Charles tried to fill the vacuum left from losing John's love by replacing it with John Bennet's.[45]

We see similar sentiments in Charles when John eventually married Mary Vazeille in February 1751. Having been thwarted by Charles in his first attempt at marriage, John disregarded his pact with his brother and did not consult him when Mary came into the picture. John indicated his intentions to marry, but provided no details about the identity of his intended. Ironically, John might have profited from consulting Charles about Mary. Charles evidently saw something in Mary Vazeille, which John had missed. Following his first contact with Mary Vazeille at Ned Perronet's home a year earlier, she impressed him as ". . . woman of a sorrowful spirit" and Charles noted this in his journal.[46] Evidently, he saw something in Mary, which had registered in him a negative opinion. When Charles discovered the identity of the woman his brother intended to marry, his response was quite dramatic. Charles wrote in his journal:

> Sat., February 2d. My brother, returned from Oxford, sent for and told me *he was resolved to marry!* I was thunderstruck, and could only answer, he had given me the first blow, and his marriage would come like the *coup de grace*. Trusty Ned Perronet followed, and told me, the person was Mrs. Vazeille! one of whom I had never had the least suspicion. I refused his company to the chapel,

44. Baker, "Investigating."
45. Lloyd, *Charles Wesley.*
46. Wesley, C., *The Journal,* Vol. 2, 62.

and retired to mourn with my faithful Sally. I groaned all the day, and several following ones, under my own and the people's burden. I could eat no pleasant food, nor preach, nor rest, either by night or by day.[47]

Evidently, John's marriage provoked a significant negative impact in Charles. His previously formed negative opinion of Mary's personality as well as his concerns for Methodism likely provoked this reaction. However, as suggested by other evidence, John's marriage represented a personal loss, one felt so deeply, it estranged him from his brother and his new wife. On Sunday, February 24th, 1751, Charles noted in his journal entry how one Mr. Blackwell had to drag him to his new sister-in-law. Apparently, a few days later on Wednesday Feb. 27, Charles had begun to unthaw towards his brother and sister-in-law. In his entry for that day, he noted that John came to the chapel house with Mrs. Wesley and his gladness at seeing him. He even saluted Mrs. Wesley and stayed to hear his brother preach.[48] By March 15, the reconciliation seemed almost complete as captured in his language in his journal. Charles wrote, "I called on my dear sister; kissed and assured her I was perfectly reconciled to her, and to my brother."[49] A few days later on March 19, Charles brought his wife and his new sister-in-law together, assuring the latter of his love and respect.

But one of the most revealing indicators of the impact of John's marriage on Charles came from a poem the latter wrote following his brother's marriage. He titled the poem "Ah Woe is Me, A Man of Woe" and wrote it in 10 stanzas: I have reproduced some revealing stanzas, namely stanzas 3, 5, 7, and 8 below:

> Too happy in His Love I was,
> *I was*—but I submit!
> Irreparable is the Loss,
> The ruin is compleat.

> The dearest Sharer of my heart,
> Ah! Whither is he fled!
> My Friend, whom death could never p[ar]t,
> To me is doubly dead.

47. Ibid. 78.
48. Ibid.
49. Ibid. 79.

My other Self, but more belov'd
In youth, in manhood tried,
Faithful for 30 winters prov'd,
Is ravish'd from my side.

O what a mighty loss is mine!
The anguish who can tell,
The more than anguish, to resign
A soul, I lov'd so well.[50]

Charles also entertained rather harsh thoughts about Mary winning over John. In verse 6, he described the one who took John as possessing "soft Ephesian's charms," no doubt a reference to Mary possessing the wiles of the goddess Diana (Artemis), which she used to wrest John "to her bewitching arms" Other poems written about his brother's marriage possess the same theme of loss. For example, Charles wrote another poem titled "Why Shoud I in Unhallow'd Pain" of which the first stanza read:

Why shoud I in unhallow'd pain
My pretious Moments spend,
Or fondly for the Loss complain
Of every earthly Friend?
How can I need if still possest
Of Him my Friend above,
If every Loss secures my rest
In his Eternal Love.[51]

The poems cited, as well as others found in this unpublished poetry of Charles Wesley, clearly show how keenly he felt the loss of his brother. The verses reveal the unfathomable depth of emotion and grief Charles felt. The depth of emotions demonstrates the almost symbiotic relationship, which existed between the brothers. As Charles described it, John was his "other self but more belov'd." This description supports the lack of differentiation and corresponding enmeshment, which existed between the two. This reality in their relationship fostered in both, a profound sense of loss when the other developed an intimate relationship and subsequently married.

---

50. Kimbrough and Beckerlegge, "The Unpublished Poetry of Charles Wesley," 320.

51. Ibid., 321.

Emotional and Physical Cut Off in the Wesley Family

Besides problems related to individuation and enmeshment, one also finds many examples of emotional and physical cutoff in the Wesley family. In emotional cutoff, one detaches emotionally from a significant other. In physical cutoff, one literally takes flight, also called fugue, from the significant other.[52] Emotional and physical cutoff derives logically from too much closeness and represents an effort to break free. Moreover, lack of differentiation or fusion can fuel cutoff and later revert back to fusion.[53] Because fusion and cutoff represent the extreme ends of family functioning, wild pendulum swings from one extreme to the other often result. In a sense, emotional or physical cutoff represents a desperate, though unsuccessful, attempt to address problems of fusion and enmeshment, and to individuate.[54] One of the first examples of cutoff in the Wesley extended family occurred in the relationship between Susanna and her father Samuel Annesley Sr. Perhaps the seeds for a possible rift between her and her father were sown when at age thirteen Susanna renounced his dissenting faith, embracing the Church of England. Years later, her marriage to a rigid, Church of England clergyman, who had also rejected his dissenting faith, would not have helped to better her relationship with her father.[55] In spite of this reasoning, no tangible evidence supports an early rift. Nevertheless, as indicated earlier in this book, Samuel Annesley Senior did exclude Susanna and the Wesleys from his will. Years later, Susanna's brother Samuel Annesley Junior broke his promise to the Epworth Wesleys, and also cut them off with a shilling.[56] In doing so, he replicated his father's pattern, which was likely influenced by the business tensions he experienced with Samuel Wesley. In my opinion, these two instances stand as early examples of cutoff.

On a related note, some controversy exists over the epitaphs, which adorned Susannah's Wesley's tomb. Her original epitaph read: "Mrs. Susannah Wesley, The Youngest and last surviving daughter of Dr. Samuel

52. Blessing, "Murray Bowen's.

53. Titleman, "Emotional Cutoff."

54. Bowen, "Differentiation"; Nichols, *Family Therapy*; Nichols and Schwartz, *Family Therapy*; Skowron, "Differentiation of Self."

55. Dallimore, *Susanna*.

56. Maser, *Story of John Wesley's Sisters*.

Annesley."[57] Because her original epitaph did not include her marriage to Samuel Wesley, Abelove[58] spoke of John Wesley blanking out his parent's marriage. Later in 1828, Susanna's epitaph was changed to include a reference to her husband Samuel and then read:

> Here lies the body of
> MRS. SUSANNAH WESLEY
> Widow of the Rev. Samuel Wesley, M.A.
> (late Rector of Epworth, in Lincolnshire,)
> who died July 23, 1742.
> Aged 73 years.
> She was the Youngest Daughter of the
> Rev. Samuel Annesley, D. D., ejected by the Act
> of Uniformity from the Rectory of St. Giles's,
> Cripplegate, August 24, 1662.
> She was the Mother of nineteen Children,
> of Whom the most eminent were the
> REV. JOHN and CHARLES WESLEY;
> the former of whom was under God the
> Founder of the Societies of the People-
> called Methodists.[59]

The new wording on Susanna Wesley's Epitaph, Bunhill Field, City Road, London, from a photo taken by Kenneth A. Boyd, Ph.D. Used with permission.

57. Clarke, *Memoirs*, 414.

58. Abelove, *Evangelist of Desire*.

59. Clarke, *Memoirs*, 420.

Given the cutoff by her father, I would entertain a hypothesis regarding the original epitaph different than that at which Abelove arrived. Rather than serving as an example of John mentally erasing his parent's marriage, the epitaph was likely requested by Susanna and represented her effort to reclaim in death the family heritage and connection to the father who had cut her off.

Besides this example, another significant example exists. Here I refer to the cutoff of Hetty Wesley following her escapade. Not so coincidentally, this incident replicates the previous family generational pattern: namely, estrangement and cutoff of a favored daughter from a beloved father. Like the relationship, which existed between Susanna and her father, Samuel Annesley, Hetty, too, was a favored daughter of her father, Samuel Wesley. She served as his amanuensis and was considered his beloved child.[60] But, like her mother, Susanna, whose father had cut her off in his will, Hetty experienced emotional and physical cut-off from her father for the rest of her life. Incidentally, some degree of estrangement might also have existed between Samuel and several of his daughters. Evidence from the Wesley family letters would seem to support such a conclusion. This conclusion about emotional distance between Samuel Wesley and his daughters finds its best example in Emilia. As cited in earlier parts of this book, her letters seem to contain some disdain for her father.[61]

But, cutoff can also occur within marriage relationships. In marriage, fusion often results in reactive emotional distance between marital partners, sometimes leading to physical or emotional dysfunction and marital conflict. Such problems also tend to get projected onto one or more children within a family, thereby replicating the pattern in other generations.[62] We see such patterns in Samuel and Susanna Wesley and their offspring. I have indicated some of these problems in the genogram indicated below.

As demonstrated in the genogram, many of the Wesley marriages experienced conflict and distress. Conflict, coupled with emotional and physical cutoff, characterized the marriages of Samuel and Susanna Wesley, Richard and Emilia Harper, Richard and Susanna Ellison, William and Hetty Wright, Westley and Martha Hall, and of course, John

60. Maser, *Story of John Wesley's Sisters.*

61. Wesley, E., "Letter from Lincoln to John Wesley," December 31, 1729; "Letter to John Wesley," February 9, 1730.

62. Nichols, *Family Therapy;* Nichols and Schwartz, *Family Therapy.*

and Mary Wesley. Some marital problems, including deprivation, might also have existed in the relationship between John and Anne Lambert, notwithstanding the idyllic picture presented of this relationship.[63] In my

FIGURE 6.1 Emotional and Physical Cutoff in the Wesley Marriages[64]

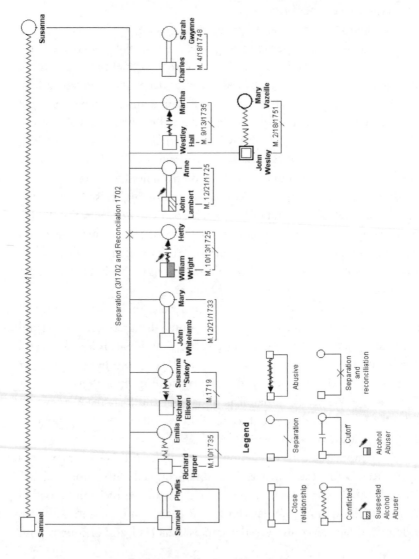

63. Maser, *Story of John Wesley's Sisters.*

64. Based primarily on Maser, *Story of John Wesley's Sisters,* and John Wesley's relationship with his wife as revealed in his correspondence. Methodist History, 32(1), 4–18.

examination of the Wesley family letters, I found several references to difficulties in Anne's life involving apparent health issues and poverty. In fact, her difficulties likely went back at least to 1731, and might have extended through the rest of her life.[65] I have discussed these issues in greater detail in an article about Anne Wesley.[66] Besides deprivation in many of the Wesley marriages, marital conflict sometimes erupted in physical and likely emotional abuse. Richard Harper, Richard Ellison, William Wright, and Westley Hall all abused their wives in some manner.[67]

But other examples of cutoff exist. For example, following the death of Mary Wesley in 1734, her husband, John Whitelamb, complained of being ostracized by the family. Apparently, the whole family, with the exception of John, distanced from him.[68] Perhaps the disconnection resulted from Whitelamb's past disfavor with the Wesleys. Although he had married the crippled Mary Wesley, he had not endeared himself to the family. Earlier, he had written a rather unflattering letter about Kezia Wesley to Westley Hall, who had courted Kezia while engaged to her sister Martha (whom he would eventually marry). These actions appropriately drew the ire of the Wesleys. Besides this, while pre-engaged to Mary, Whitelamb had pursued a relationship with one Miss Betty. This infuriated Susanna and she communicated her displeasure in a letter to John. In it Susanna laid out the moral flaw she found in Whitelamb.

> My principal business with you was about Whitelamb, to reprimand your great caution in not informing me what his moral character is, and about his intrigue at Medley. Had you let me know of the looseness of his principles and his disreputable practices; I would never have forwarded his going into Orders, neither would I have suffered him to renew his addresses to Molly after such a notorious violation of his promise to her . . .[69]

Susanna evidently did not approve of the marriage of her daughter Mary (referred to in the family as Molly) but was apparently overruled by her husband, Samuel. Her disapproval appears in the following excerpt from the same letter indicated above:

65. Lambert, "Letter to John Wesley"; Wesley, S. J., "Letter to Susanna Wesley," 3 July 1731; "Letter from Salisbury," April 29, 1736.

66. Headley, "Anne Wesley."

67. Maser, *Story of John Wesley's Sisters.*

68. Ibid.

69. Wesley, Susanna, "Letter to John Wesley," January 1, 1734.

> . . . I was extremely unwilling Molly should ever marry at all. But Molly, who was very fond of him to the last degree, was of another mind; and persuaded him to write to Robinson and show me the letter, I did not much approve it because he seemed to justify those vile practices, which I thought he ought to have condemned, yet to satisfy her importunity I permitted them to go on. Whitelamb wrote to ask your father leave to marry his daughter, which Mr. Wesley gave him, and on St. Thomas' Day married they were at Epworth by Mr. Horberry; sore against my will, but my consent was never asked, and your father, Bro: Wesley being for the match, I said nothing against it to them, only laboured what I could to dissuade Molly from it, but the flesh and the devil were to me, I could not prevail.[70]

Besides these indiscretions, John Whitelamb evidently possessed leanings towards deism and later became enamored with Catholicism. Whatever the reasons, following Mary's death, Whitelamb evidently felt and thought the Wesleys had cut him off.[71] One can even point to another example from Kezia, the youngest Wesley sibling. As I implied earlier, Westley Hall courted her and proposed to her while engaged to her sister Martha. After the marriage between Westley Hall and Martha, Kezia lived with them for a period of time. The brothers greatly disapproved of this arrangement (and rightly so). In reaction, her oldest brother, Samuel Jr., cut her off for a period of time.[72]

Although I could cite other examples of cutoff in the Wesley family, I conclude by discussing the estrangement, which developed between John and Charles following the Grace Murray affair. Moreover, estrangement between the brothers continued when John married Mary Vazeille. But the estrangement and cutoff between them expressed itself most poignantly in the aftermath of the Grace Murray affair. John Wesley, himself, provided an account in his journal entry for October 5, 1749:

> Thurs 5, 1749: About eight one came in from Newcastle, and told us, 'They were married on Tuesday.' My brother came an hour after. I felt no anger, yet I did not desire to see him. But Mr. Whitefield constrained me. After a few words had passed, he accosted me with, 'I renounce all intercourse with you, but what I would have with an heathen or a publican.' I felt little emotion. It was only adding a drop of water to a drowning man, yet I calmly accepted

70. Ibid.

71. Maser, *Story of John Wesley's Sisters.*

72. Ibid.

his renunciation, and acquiesced therein. Poor Mr. Whitefield and
John Nelson burst into tears. They prayed, cried and entreated, till
the storm passed away. We could not speak, but only fell on each
other's neck.[73]

This account provides many interesting insights into the dynamics
of the brother's estrangement. Though John did not acknowledge anger,
his brother's action sufficiently moved him enough so that he refused
his brother's presence. John apparently had become numb, and George
Whitefield had to persuade him to see his brother. Even then, Charles,
as impulsive as ever, burned with anger and expressed it in a classic
pronouncement of cutoff, *"I renounce all intercourse with you, but what
I would have with an heathen or a publican."* On that occasion, the brothers attempted reconciliation, but their relationship was never the same.
According to one author, great tension existed between the brothers and
they displaced it in their bitter debates over Methodism's future.[74]

Following John's marriage about a year and a half later, we see a
similar distancing in Charles when he discovered John's resolve to marry.
I quoted Charles' words earlier in this chapter, but reference the experience here for review. The news apparently threw Charles off kilter. He
described himself as "thunderstruck." Apparently borrowing from duel-
ing imagery, Charles saw the news of his brother's resolve to marry as a
striking of the first blow. The marriage itself would serve as the deadly
"coup de grace," to pierce his chest and wound him mortally. Even more
alarming for Charles was his discovery of Mrs. Mary Vazeille as John's
intended. In a sign of physical cutoff, he refused his brother's company to
the chapel, retiring to mourn and grieve with his wife, Sally.[75]

Hopefully, these examples provide sufficient proof of the pattern of
physical and emotional cutoff in the Wesley family. These tensions and
estrangements became the price exacted for being as close as they were.
When a member's decisions, choices, or actions differed from the unspoken family rule, cutoff followed. The area of difference varied. Sometimes
it was disagreement over the rightful king. At other times, it involved
deviation from family mores, or ill-advised relationships. But the unspoken family rule about sameness seemed to frequently lend itself to cutoff
when family members deviated. As I have indicated, this likely traced its

73. Curnock, "The Journal," Vol. 3, 439.

74. Lloyd, *Charles Wesley.*

75. Wesley, C., *The Journal.*

origin back to their ancestry. I have at least traced its possible presence in Samuel Annesley's disinheriting his daughter Susanna. From here, it continued in Samuel and Susanna Wesley and their progeny.

Perhaps it is good to end this discussion with the example of Charles' cutoff from his brother John. Some have characterized Charles as bearing the rash and impulsive traits of his father, Samuel.[76] Not surprisingly, Charles and his father provide the two clearest examples of cutoff in behavior and language. Years before, Samuel said to his wife, "*You and I must part; for if we have two kings, we must have two beds.*"[77] Then he retreated from her bed and eventually left the home. Years later, Charles would speak just as clearly and rashly when he said to John, "*I renounce all intercourse with you, but what I would have with an heathen or a publican,*" and retreated from relationship with his brother. Apples do not fall very far from the proverbial family tree!

Relationship Interference in the Wesley Family

Among the Wesleys, physical and emotional cutoff often followed previous interference in another member's life. Such was the case in Charles' interference in John Wesley's relationship with Grace Murray. One author provided this revealing statement about their interference in each others' lives:

> It is a melancholy fact that so much of the unhappiness of the Wesley family was caused by their interference in each other's love affairs. The sisters let each other alone. But the Rector and his three sons all interfered with marriages on occasion and not always wisely.[78]

In his study of the lives of the Wesley sisters, Frederick Maser[79] largely agreed with this assessment. He noted the disharmony, which often existed between them, and connected it to their interference in each other's lives and loves. Unfortunately, this interference often created havoc for family members. However, although I agree with the judgment relative to interference in intimate relationships, I disagree with Edwards when he limited interference to the men in the family. Evidence supports interference by their mother, Susanna, and by her youngest daughter, Kezia. For example,

76. Edwards, *Sons to Samuel*.
77. Clarke, *Memoirs*, 165.
78. Edwards, *Family Circle*, 139.
79. Maser, *Story of John Wesley's Sisters*.

Susanna influenced her eldest son, Samuel, to exert pressure on Emilia to break off a relationship with Richard Leybourne, the evident love of her life.[80] This loss created emotional havoc for Emilia, as evidenced by her letters to John where she spoke about Leybourne and her grief at losing him.[81] Kezia and her mother, Susanna, also indirectly interfered in Mary's relationship with John Whitelamb. Kezia was the person who likely leaked a story about John Whitelamb's indiscretions with a woman named Betty. To even the score, Whitelamb later wrote a letter denouncing Kezia's character to her suitor, Westley Hall.[82] However, for the most part, it seems fair to say the women most often interfered *indirectly* in the romantic break-ups, whereas the Wesley men frequently intervened *directly*.

The Wesley men might have thought they had good reason for interfering in the relationships of their females. For the most part, the Wesley women often involved themselves with men who turned out to be scoundrels. Moreover, their cultural context encouraged patriarchal habits, where men served as the primary decision makers for the women in their lives. Related to this dynamic, the Wesley men saw themselves as the providers and protectors of their sisters, and likely saw their interference in this light, though the results often proved disastrous. However, the men did not simply interfere with their sister's relationships; one of the most blatant examples of interference in romantic relationships involved Charles marrying off John's intended, Grace Murray, to John Bennet. As we have indicated in earlier chapters, Charles often fell under the sway of his elder brother, John.[83] However, in this case, the roles switched. Charles became John's protector and thus foiled the latter's relationship with Grace. His behavior likely flowed from anxiety about John's suitability for marriage. Thus, when George Whitefield suggested the brothers marry, Charles adamantly pleaded for John's exemption.[84] In fairness to Charles, John himself entertained similar thoughts about his suitability for marriage. For several years John believed himself incapable of keeping a wife and thought himself ill suited to handle the complicated temptations of married life.[85] Charles likely knew this.

80. Ibid.

81. Wesley, E., "Letter to John Wesley," April 7, 1725.; "Letter from Lincoln," December 31, 1729.

82. Maser, *Story of John Wesley's Sisters.*

83. Lloyd, *Charles Wesley.*

84. Ibid.

85. Curnock, "The Journal"; Heitzenrater, *Elusive.*

We can relate the pattern of interference to the formation of emotional triangles. In chapter 1, I defined emotional triangles as involving the introduction of a third party or thing into a two-person relationship. Triangles usually develop from anxiety within a dyadic relation and consciously or unconsciously serve to resolve tensions in that relationship. Paradoxically, in many cases, the development of the triangle normally blocks resolution between the pair.[86] In the interference pattern in the Wesley family, anxiety, which provoked the formation of triangles, often came from outside the dyad. This does not mean anxiety did not exist in the two-person relationship. Rather, it means anxiety also exhibited itself in persons outside the dyad. This often led such persons to interject themselves into the relationship, barging their way into the relationship without invitation. Thus, in the break up of Emilia's relationship with Richard Leybourne, Susanna, along with other members of the family, became anxious enough to intervene and end the relationship. These interference patterns and their consequences are indicated in Figure 6.2 below. In the figure, I have not tried to capture all the specific persons who interfered, but the relationships in which interference occurred. I have also not tried to capture all the instances of interference in romantic relationships. I have merely endeavored to highlight those instances, which occurred in the identified marriages, although at times, I make oblique reference to other instances. I have also sought to capture those marriages in which the family member did not seek permission or consult members in the family. By these strategies, I hope to illustrate the general pattern within the family. The reader who wishes to investigate other instances of interference might consult Maser's story of the Wesley's sisters.[87] In my estimation, Maser did a good job in detailing the several instances of interference. Based on the genogram, several observations merit comment about the interference pattern. In making these comments, I will also provide specific examples of the how the interference functioned and the consequences which derived from it. Besides Charles' interference into John's relationship with Grace Murray, the most dramatic example occurred when Samuel Sr. forced Hetty to marry William Wright.[88] One might understand his desire for Hetty's marriage especially given her pregnancy while yet unmarried.

86. Bowen, *Family Therapy*; Nichols, *Family Therapy*; Nichols and Schwartz, *Family Therapy*.

87. Maser, *Story of John Wesley's Sisters*.

88. Baker, "Investigating"; Maser, *Story of John Wesley's Sisters*.

But, even before Hetty's escapade, Samuel had acted to squash her relationship with an interested lawyer and with his own amanuensis, John Romley.[89] Besides these, several other examples existed including John Wesley's own interference in Emilia's relationship with a physician, likely because of his Quaker faith.[90]

FIGURE 6.2 Relationship Interference in the Wesley Family[91]

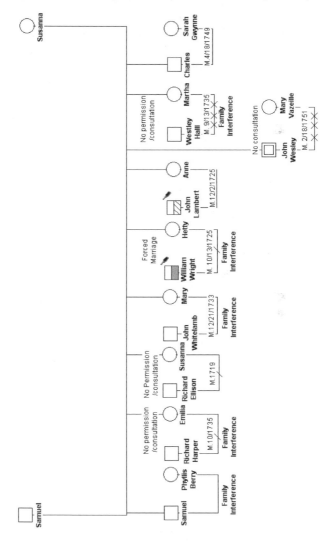

89. Maser, *Story of John Wesley's Sisters.*

90. Ibid.

91. Based primarily on Maser, *Story of John Wesley's Sisters.*

We catch some glimpses of John's influence in the matter from a letter written to him by Emilia in February 1734:

> Dear Brother,
>
> You doubtless have long expected a letter from me, but to tell you the plain truth, in your last, you set me a lesson, so hard and full of difficulty that it has puzzled me almost ever since, at least till within this last fortnight, to break off an intimate friendship with a most agreeable companion. Unprovoked was such a thing as I scarce knew how to put into practice. Again it seemed mighty convenient to break off the correspondence sooner or later and what time is so convenient as the present. Thus wavering an uncertain I remained one week conversing, another refusing to speak or to see him, till the week before last when chance furnished me with sufficient matter to turn the scale, which before <u>you</u> had brought me to an equality.[92]

In most cases, the interference birthed negative results at several levels. First, the interference normally ended the relationship and led to a cascading mass of negative emotions about the loss. Earlier, I mentioned the emotional repercussions in John Wesley following the loss of Grace Murray. The same proved true for Emilia when family interference disrupted her relationship with Leybourne. The loss brought ongoing and prolonged grief for Emilia and she wrote about the pain of her loss in several letters to John Wesley.[93] Second, following the interference, having experienced the grief and disappointment of a lost relationship, the Wesley sibling eventually entered another relationship. In some cases, it appeared the new relationship derived from a reactive response to the previous loss. Moreover, the family member often kept the existence of the new relationship secret or provided few details about it. Neither did they seek permission or consult with any family member. In essence, they maintained a degree of secrecy to protect their relationships from interference. For example, Robert Harper courted Emilia, and though she was seriously considering marriage to him, she did not confide in her family. Eventually, John Wesley, himself, performed this marriage prior

---

92. Wesley, E., "Letter to John Wesley," February 7, 1734.

93. Wesley, E., "Letter to John Wesley," April 7, 1725; "Letter from Lincoln," December 31, 1729.; "Letter to John Wesley," February 9, 1730; "Letter to John Wesley," October 5, 1730.

to leaving for Georgia. Similarly, Martha Wesley did not seek permission or consult any family member.[94]

If these were the only ramifications of interference, it would not merit much discussion. However, disastrous results usually followed the new relationships formed in the wake of interference and disruption of a previous relationship.[95] Of course, although the interference seems indirectly related, one cannot say the interference directly caused the unhappy circumstances in subsequent relationships. One can only hypothesize about how this indirect influence occurred, but it also might have occurred in the following manner: The interference demonstrated in a previous relationship inspired a rebound effect into a bad relationship. This could have occurred because the new relationship derived from an emotionally reactive response to the previous loss and was not well thought out or considered. Even if this conclusion proves untrue, triangulation expressed through interference in sibling relationships usually spelled trouble for subsequent relationships.

Incidentally, new and disastrous relationship did not always flow from the loss of a previous relationship. Sometimes, some great disappointment fostered the disastrous relationship. This proved true in the case of Susanna, the second daughter, named after her mother and called 'Sukey' by the family. Her Uncle Samuel Annesley had promised her some sort of inheritance but the gift never came, and she too entered a disastrous marriage. According to one source, she married Ellison "... in pique because the gift promised by her Uncle Annesley had not been forthcoming."[96] Apparently, the loss of the inheritance made a reportedly wealthy Richard Ellison, an attractive prospect. Additionally, she might have pursued the marriage because of the poverty conditions in her home life. Whatever the reason, she reactively entered a relationship with Ellison. According to the record, she practically threw herself at him. But Richard Ellison was a coarse and vulgar fellow. In a letter to her brother, Samuel Annesley Junior, written on her birthday, January 20, 1721, Susanna Wesley provided an assessment of Richard Ellison. She also linked the marriage to Sukey's reaction to an unkind letter from him:

> My second Daughter Suky a pretty woman, and worthy a better
> fate, when your last unkind letters she perceived that all her hopes

94. Maser, *Story of John Wesley's Sisters.*

95. Ibid.

96. Ibid. 32.

in you were frustrated, rashly threw herself away upon a man (if man he may be called that is little inferior to the Apostate Angels in Wickedness) that is not only her Plague but a constant Affliction to the Family.[97]

Others in the family shared similar assessments about Richard Ellison. Samuel Jr. said of him, "I wonder at nothing in relation to Dick, who if I mistake him not, does not desire to have it thought, he has any religion; good nature or good manners . . ."[98]

Richard Ellison would physically abuse Sukey for much of her married life until she left him. On one occasion, he beat her within an inch of her life, even when she was with child.[99] Her plight appeared so desperate, John Wesley considered taking her and her children to Georgia with him.[100] Ironically, Richard Ellison, whom Sukey married because of his perceived wealth, lost it and became a financial piranha on the Wesley family. In one letter to his mother, Samuel Junior warned his mother never to trust Ellison with the tithe.[101] In another letter, Emilia noted, "Dick I found deeply engaged, both on my father's account and his own, that is, he has given bond, and accepted bills of my father's creditors as far as his rent went, and owes besides money enough on his own account, that were he to die tomorrow I don't believe he would leave one shilling behind him when his debts were paid."[102] Sukey's condition only improved with separation from Richard Ellison. In fact, many of the unhappy marriages in the Wesley family only found relief through separation or cutoff.

97. Wesley, Susanna, "Letter from Epworth."

98. Wesley, S. J., "Letter to John Wesley," 6 January 1728.

99. Wesley, E., "Letter to John Wesley," February 9, 1730.

100. Maser, Story of John Wesley's Sisters.

101. Wesley, S. J., "Letter to Susanna Wesley," 3 July 1731.

102. Wesley, E., "Letter to John Wesley," March 14, 1730.

chapter 7

Family Marriage Patterns and the Influence
on John Wesley's Intimate Relationships

FAMILIES OFTEN SHAPE RELATIONSHIPS after their own likeness and image. If this is correct, as I believe it is, the family legacies and ambivalences created by disastrous family marriages would exert profound influence on yet unmarried family members. The relational patterns would likely influence its members in at least two ways. First, the patterns could contribute to some ambivalence about marriage in unmarried members. Second, they could exert influence on the kind of relationships they formed. I believe this is true of John Wesley and his relationships. As indicated in the previous chapter, a lack of individuation and concomitant enmeshment characterized many Wesley family relationships. Additionally, family members resorted to emotional and physical distancing from each other, especially when members departed from established family norms. Finally, I discussed a pattern of interference in which family members triangulated themselves into the relationships of other members, often leading to disappointment and loss. As a reaction to previous losses, some members formed new relationships while maintaining secretiveness, or at least, did not consult with other members or seek their permission when beginning new intimate relationships. Invariably, the relationships formed in this manner produced disastrous results, including physical and emotional abuse, and even cutoff.

How might these and other family patterns exhibited in relationships connect to John Wesley's intimate relationships? In my opinion, it is highly unlikely they failed to influence his relationships. The problem is to figure out the manner in which they influenced his relationships. I will largely do this by trying to apply the family relationship patterns observed to his intimate relationships. Consistent with this manner of thinking, I propose the following hypothesis: Wesley's relationships with the three women for whom he entertained marital notions, conformed in many respects to patterns seen in the family. More specifically, the patterns in the unhappy Wesley marriages fit those evident in John's marriage to Mary Vazeille.

To begin to lay out arguments for this hypothesis, I will review Wesley's relationships with Sophy Hopkey, Grace Murray, and Mary Vazeille. However, I will place the major emphasis on the latter two, since the connection between them illustrate well the influence of the family patterns. Throughout this book, I have provided glimpses into these relationships on different occasions. I will not rehash all of these details but will instead focus on additional salient aspects, which support the replication of the family relationship patterns. Additionally, rather than treat these relationships separately, I will consider them together as I believe this approach will more likely reveal the relational patterns. In focusing on these three relationships, I do not discount the possibility of earlier romantic relationships.[1] However, in these three, Wesley seriously entertained thoughts of marriage, and as we know, contracted a marriage with Mary Vazeille. In Figure 7.1, I have provided a genogram of these relationships, along with other information, which I consider critical to the discussion. The genogram raises several interesting issues that merit some discussion prior to delving into the connection of the family patterns to his intimate relationships. Perhaps this discussion will help lay some groundwork for further understanding of Wesley's intimate relationships and his own unique patterns in fostering these personal contacts. I begin the discussion by devoting some time to the shared characteristics evident in these three women, beginning with the developmental challenges each faced.

Developmental Challenges in Wesley's Three Loves

Although different in age and life circumstances, the women Wesley loved shared similar characteristics worth considering. First, each grappled with various horizontal stressors. As some might recall, horizontal stressors involve the developmental pressures persons face as they move across time. Sophy Hopkey experienced her own developmental concerns. She was a young woman in her late teens living with a maternal aunt and the latter's husband. Apparently, difficulties in her home made it a complicated

---

1. Dobree, *Biography*; Rack, *Reasonable Enthusiast*; Rogal, "John Wesley Takes a Wife."

FIGURE 7.1 John Wesley's Three Intimate Relationships[2]

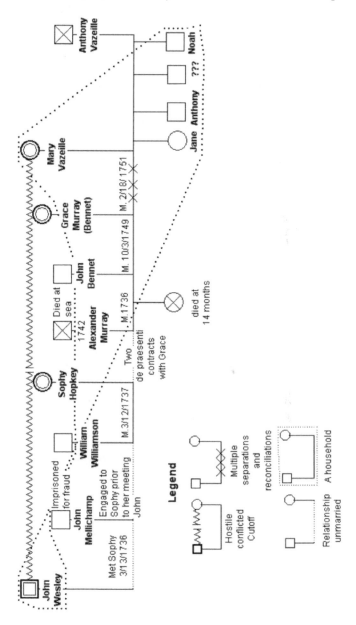

2. Information compiled from various sources including Clarke, *Memoirs*; Collins, "John Wesley's Relationship with his Wife," Rogal, *Susanna Annesley Wesley*.

place to live. Her Uncle Causton, a magistrate at Savannah, apparently wanted relief from further trouble with her and was only too ready to marry her off. At one time, when she had moved to Frederica, she did not wish to return to her uncle's house. She felt alone, especially in Frederica where she had no one to trust except the Hirds. Besides this, she experienced her own relationship difficulties; she was engaged to or promised to one Tom Mellichamp, a man imprisoned for fraud. While she could not marry her intended or chose not to, her friends, such as Ms. Fosset, were approaching marriage.[3] John Wesley evidently carried some concern for her during her stay at Frederica, and accordingly, he wrote his brother Charles, who lived in Frederica, asking him to guard her and watch over her.[4]

Grace Murray also faced her own developmental difficulties. She was a widowed woman of about thirty-two years when she connected with Wesley. She had become widowed after six years of marriage when her husband, Alexander Murray, drowned at sea.[5] She evidently desired to remarry. Given her age and the implications for childbearing, I suspect there existed in her some sense of urgency to remarry. Besides, aside from losing her husband, Grace had also lost a child from her first marriage when the child died at 14 months. Having lost these two important figures in her life, I suspect there existed within her a heightened interest to replace both her lost husband and child. Apparently, Grace Murray was a sensitive and compassionate soul. She became known for nursing preachers, in Newcastle, who became ill. Conveniently, many single preachers, including John Wesley and John Bennet, became sick at the Newcastle Orphan House where Grace resided.[6] Grace's sensitive nature sometimes provoked worry about matters beyond her control. For example, while living in Newcastle, a Christian man named John Brydon fell in love with her, and although no engagement existed, some assumed she would marry him. In 1743, Grace left Newcastle and moved to London. Upon her return, she discovered John had married and left the faith. Grace took this news rather badly, not because of his marriage, but because she held her-

3. Curnock, "The Journal."
4. Southey, *The Life of John Wesley.*
5. Curnock, "The Journal."
6. Dobree, *Biography.*

self responsible for his loss of faith. From her distorted perspective, John Brydon lost his faith because she had not married him. Consequently, she fell into deep depression, thought she were headed for hell, and almost lost her own faith in the process. She continued in this state of misperceived culpability and depression for two years.[7] Coincidentally, Grace's depression might have been linked to another possible mental condition. One author, who noted the Brydon episode, also mentioned the presence of mood swings in her memoirs. This led the author to conclude she might have suffered with bipolar disorder, or what is popularly called manic depression.[8]

Significantly, a similar experience occurred in her relationship with John Bennet. Bennet tried to persuade Grace of God's will that she marry him. At one point, torn between Bennet and Wesley, but desiring the latter, she told Wesley, "How can you think I love anyone better than I love you! I love you a thousand times better than I ever loved John Bennet in my life. *But I am afraid, If I don't marry him, he'll run mad.*"[9] (Italics mine). The last statement caught my attention. It reminded me of Grace's concerns and depression when Brydon lost his faith. She evidently felt a weight of responsibility for Brydon's failed faith. She felt the same level of responsibility, inappropriately so, for Bennet's mental state. If she did not marry him, she would hold herself culpable for any resulting madness. No wonder she vacillated to such a degree between the two and accepted proposals from Bennet on two occasions as well as agreed to two de praesenti contracts with John Wesley.[10]

Perhaps Wesley preferred widows as he formed his next relationship with Mary Vazeille, a forty-one year old widow with four children from her previous marriage to Anthony Vazeille. Mr. Vazeille had amassed a sizable fortune through his merchant business, and upon his death, left his wife and children in good financial shape. He reputedly left her some £10,000 to be received at £300 pounds per year. In addition, he left her a London home on Threadneedle Street and a country home in Wandsworth.[11] Moreover, Mr. Vazeille apparently deferred to her and

7. Tyerman, *Life and Times.*

8. Valentine, *John Bennet.*

9. Tyerman, *Life and Times*, Vol. 2, 51.

10. Ward and Heitzenrater, *The Works*, Vol. 18.

11. Rogal, "Wesley Takes a Wife"; Tyerman, *Life and Times.*

catered to her varied needs. In contrast to her previous life, life with John exposed her to demanding travel, plus deprivations and inconveniences.[12] Moreover, John's itinerant schedule left him precious little time to attend to the demands of marital life. Besides, according to Wesley, he was ill suited to the marital state; he lacked the graces and virtues required of a married man, and evidently did not adjust well to its demands. Moreover, Mary carried the responsibility for her young children. This reality restricted the possibility of the constant travel expected of an itinerant preacher's wife. These considerations contributed to a difficult marital journey with John Wesley.[13]

Relationships, Anxiety and Triangulation in Wesley's Three Loves

Second, besides the developmental issues present in their lives, Wesley's romantic interests shared another characteristic. Each had experienced prior relationships; Sophy had been engaged, and both Grace and Mary had experienced marriage. Past relationships such as these can often influence how one functions in present attachments. For example, one must wonder if the demands of itinerant ministry on Mary drew unfavorable comparisons between John Wesley and Anthony Vazeille, with John coming out the loser. But even in the present, each woman experienced relationships, which could contribute to potential problems in their relationships with a man like Wesley. Mary Vazeille carried responsibility for her children, and their illnesses made the task more difficult.[14] Sophy and Grace each had real and potential suitors, and their presence detracted from Wesley's own relationship with them. Sophy expressed commitment to Tom Mellichamp, who lurked as a somewhat shadowy figure waiting in the wings. Later, William Williamson would enter the picture and wrest his way into Sophy's affection, hurriedly escorting her to the altar. In the case of Grace Murray, John Bennet actively competed for her affections, contributing to constant vacillation between him and John Wesley. In short, each of Wesley's relationships possessed parties who could and would become triangulated into their bond with him.

---

12. Tyerman, *Life and Times*, Vol. 2.

13. Ibid.

14. Rogal, "Wesley Takes a Wife."

The possibility for triangulation not only existed in Wesley's romantic interests, the possibilities also existed elsewhere. Charles Wesley represents one person who became triangulated into John Wesley's relationships, and indeed, he involved himself in various ways in John's relationship with both Grace Murray and Mary Vazeille. Moreover, though not in a romantic sense, other women became triangulated into John's relationship with Grace and Mary. At least, at different times, both women falsely believed John was romantically involved with other women.[15] But one can triangulate people as well as things. Given this reality, one might persuasively argue for John's triangulation of his ministry work into his relationship with Mary. In fact, it is not too far a stretch to say Wesley triangulated ministry into his relationship with each woman. His ministry would become the figurative "other woman" who would dominate his affection and his time. These realities would create challenges for the viability of these relationships, and facilitate the disastrous circumstances of his marriage.

As previously indicated, triangulation typically arises to diffuse anxiety in a twosome. I think anxiety existed at various times in all of Wesley's relationships. For example, I think John's vacillation with Sophy Hopkey created anxiety within her about her prospects for marriage. As a result, she hurriedly and precipitously rushed into a relationship with William Williamson. Furthermore, it appears possible her aunt and uncle became anxious about her possibility for marriage, leading to them to agree to Williamson's request for her hand in marriage. Mr. Causton had practically offered Sophy to Mr. Wesley but he never finalized the arrangement.[16] Given his, and Mrs. Causton's, concerns about trouble with Sophy, marriage seemed a good option to relieve them of their worries. A proposal from John Wesley would have squelched such concerns, but it never came. William Williamson's proposal of marriage was the next best option, and they took it.

Similarly, we see evidence for anxiety in both widows. When Grace experienced anxiety about the security of her ties to John, she distanced from him and moved towards John Bennet. Sometimes she became anxious when she heard gossip or rumors associating John Wesley with other

---

15. Collins, "John Wesley's Relationship"; Edwards, *Astonishing Youth*; Heitzenrater, *Elusive*; Maser, "Only Marriage"; Tyerman, *Life and Times*.

16. Curnock, "The Journal"; Dobree, *Biography*.

women such as Molly Francis.[17] Such instances presumably gave rise to a belief that John was less likely to marry her. Here too, she would turn to John Bennet.[18] Mary's numerous separations from John after she married him can be attributed to her anxieties and jealousies. Given her overly jealous and suspicious nature, she, too, readily believed rumors about his relationships with other women. Additionally, her fertile imagination, fueled by anxiety, fostered her own allegations of John's wrongdoing. Of course, John's behaviors, such as his numerous correspondences to women including Sarah Ryan and Sarah Crosby, though innocent, did not help matters.[19] Her viewing of these letters, initially with John's consent, made matters worse. Although the letters became a source of tension in their relationship, one letter was especially troublesome. In this letter, written by Mrs. Crosby to John Wesley, she openly criticized Mrs. Wesley, and as to be expected, Mrs. Wesley saw it as a personal attack.[20] All hell broke loose!

The Role of Travel and Illness in Wesley's Relationships

Third, in each of John Wesley's relationships, illness seems to have played a critical role in the formation. At some point in the relationship, each woman nursed him to health.[21] Such occasions provided a respite from ministry and time to consider the fairer sex. Speaking of Grace Murray, one Wesley writer observed, ". . . his enforced leisure gave him more appreciative eyes for his housekeeper, who also served as his nurse."[22] Following the heartrending loss of Grace Murray, the same author noted a similar pattern in John Wesley's contact with Mary Vazeille and wrote, "As for the bereft John Wesley, yet another convalescence gave him leisure to study yet another widow who used a gentle hand in nursing him, and to whom he proposed marriage."[23] From my perspective, such occasions of illness provided an opportunity for Wesley to see these women in caring

17. Baker, "Wesley's First Marriage"; Maser, "Only Marriage."

18. Telford, *The Letters*; Tyerman, *Life and Times*, Vol. 2.

19. Brown, *Women*; Collins, "John Wesley's Relationship"; Heitzenrater, *Elusive*; Maser, "Only Marriage."

20. Brown, *Women*; Collins, "John Wesley's Relationship."

21. Baker, "Wesley's First Marriage"; Coe, *Wesley and Marriage*; Dobree, *Biography*; Ethridge, *Strange Fires*; Heitzenrater, *Elusive*; Telford, *The Life of John Wesley*.

22. Baker, "Wesley's First Marriage," 177.

23. Ibid., 188.

roles. This likely helped him address an early belief that he could not find someone as caring as his mother.[24]

Wesley also traveled early on with at least two of his romantic interests, namely Sophy Hopkey and Grace Murray. Wesley's travel with Miss Sophy involved a week's travel from Frederica to Savannah.[25] During this occasion, Mr. Wesley became even more enamored with her and found his resolve not to marry severely shaken. He inquired about her relationship with Tommy Mellichamp and discovered she had promised to marry him or no one at all. In response, his words slipped out before his mind could censor them, "Miss Sophy, I should think myself happy if I was to spend my life with you."[26] Similarly, he made several lengthy travels with Grace Murray. She accompanied him on numerous preaching trips through Yorkshire, Derbyshire, and Ireland. On other occasions, she accompanied him in Bristol, London, and Newcastle.[27]

City Road Chapel (in the background directly behind Wesley's statue), London. Wesley's house is on the right. Photo by Dr. Kenneth A. Boyd. Used with permission.

As with Miss Sophy, this travel in the company of Grace Murray provided him with more than enough opportunity to consider his growing love for her. More critically, it gave him occasion to see first hand her usefulness in ministry. Out of these experiences and her nursing care, Wesley made his first oblique proposal of marriage couched in language similar to that which he had used with Miss Sophy: "If ever I marry, I think

24. Heitzenrater, *Elusive.*

25. Curnock, "The Journal"; Dobree, *Biography*; Ward and Heitzenrater, *The Works*, Vol. 18.

26. Heitzenrater, *The Works*, Vol. 18, 438.

27. Baker, "Some Observations"; Telford, *The Life of John Wesley.*

you will be the person."[28] A more direct proposal and two de praesenti contracts would follow.[29] In regard to forming relationships through illness and travel, John Wesley looked much like his brother Charles for Charles also formed his relationship with Sarah Gwynne through illness in which she nursed him to health. Additionally, Charles traveled with her and her father through Ireland for several weeks.[30] Given the brothers' hectic schedule in ministry, it would take the forced respite of illness or the convenience of travel with a female companion to awaken them to the possibilities of an intimate relationship and marriage.

The Journey to Georgia and Wesley's Relationship with Sophy Hopkey

Having discussed some common characteristic in these women, I now turn my attention to Wesley's first serious foray into the world of romantic entanglements and thoughts about matrimony. As most know, this began with Sophy Hopkey in Georgia. Accordingly, I wish to discuss this Georgian experience and what this might have meant for John Wesley. One can view his trip to Georgia from the perspective of individuation; that is, it became for him a journey of individuation—a fugue allowing him an opportunity for a fuller individuation from traditions and beliefs handed down in his family of origin and from other authority figures in his life. Journey can sometimes become a metaphor both for change and healing, even providing an opportunity to discover oneself, while breaking old allegiances and habits. It sometimes involves the tearing down of long-held traditions and beliefs, and putting them together again in a manner, which truly reflects one's new found self. Until one arrives at a more stable view of self apart from one's family of origin, one might go through a period of flux and experimentation in many areas. We often see this predicament in adolescents who journey from home to college. Sometimes they seem to quickly cast off all the vestiges of their past, and in the process become almost chameleon like, shifting and changing with each new situation. But in the process, they are slowly honing identity, keeping some things, discarding others, and forming a whole new identity. It's part of the individuation journey.

28. Baker, "Some Observations," 177.
29. Baker, "Some Observations"; Telford, The Life of John Wesley.
30. Welsey, C., The Journal, Vol. 2.

I believe Wesley's trip to Georgia represented for him an opportunity to individuate and come into his own as a person in several areas. This process would involve for him a period of flux and experimentation until he arrived at his own worked out traditions and beliefs. Significantly, one prominent authority characterized Wesley's time in Georgia as one of experimentation. In a chapter titled *The Experimental Missionary*, Frank Baker traced the shifting and flux Wesley experienced during this period.[31] Baker even described Wesley as experimenting with legalistic churchmanship. As a result, he described this period as one in which Wesley exhibited more severity and tactlessness than at any other period in his life. But even this legalistic phase shifted in Wesley. In fact, according to Baker, Wesley demonstrated a penchant for reforming the old while experimenting with the new. As a result, Wesley could tackle revision of the prayer book as well as experiment with the singing of hymns in public worship *and* the use of extemporary prayer and preaching, quite contrary to his background. In fact, years later, these habits of extemporary prayer and preaching, prompted by Susanna's expressed concerns to his brother Samuel (a good example of triangulation), would bring a sharp rebuke from the latter.[32] Besides these practices, Wesley began using laypersons, both men and women, in his pastoral work. Furthermore, outside of public worship, he organized societies for fellowship, using the Moravian practice of dividing them into bands. He even indulged in open air preaching and serving a circuit.[33] In short, during his time in Georgia, Wesley experienced various ecclesial shifts. Baker described John Wesley during this time as 'mixed.' He captured this trait poignantly in the following words:

> His desire to imitate the primitive church was by no means lessened, but the emphasis upon observance gave way markedly before an emphasis upon spirit. Wesley's faith in the authentic documentation of those observances dwindled. He continued to follow some if not most of the same practices, but with diminished zeal. Although this swing of the pendulum from undue trust in church traditions to what seemed to many an equally undue emphasis upon the mystical experiences of religion took place (as Wesley described it) "insensibly," there is little doubt that the pendulum

31. Baker, *Church of England*.
32. Wesley, S. J., "Letter to John Wesley," 16 April 1739.
33. Baker, *Church of England*.

reached the point of pause before changing direction with his closer study of Beveridge's *Synodikon*.[34]

According to Baker, Wesley's perspective on church order was truly in flux, even remaining open to further changes. No doubt, these many changes within Wesley can partly be accounted for by the many different influences under which he came in Georgia. Some of these influences came through his reading of works such as Beveridge's *Synodikon*. But it also came through his contact with the Moravian leader Spangenberg and acquaintance with their spirituality, as well as contact with Lutherans and Scottish Presbyterians.[35] But, beyond these external influences, one can also point to internal mechanisms, which might account for the experimentation and the various shifts in Wesley. I think these shifts represented the influence of the individuation process at work in Wesley; they provide ecclesial and theological evidence of the individuation process at work in him. Through these various shifts and pendulum swings, he was slowly forming his own opinions and ideas and becoming his own person albeit in a religious and professional sense.

Although this evidence for shifts in theological and ecclesial life do not necessarily prove the existence of shifts in other areas of his life, at the least, it raises the possibility that such movements were also occurring. Along with these religious shifts, I suspect Wesley began the individuation process in other areas of his life, especially his romantic life. Perhaps more than almost any other area, romantic coupling demands a journey away from one's family of origin, and becoming one's own person. It is this journey, whether metaphorical or actual, which opens the door to a maturing process necessary for marriage. In a sense, all who would mature enough to form an intimate relationship must journey away from family. Leaving the trappings of family also becomes a necessary journey if one is to bond with a spouse (Genesis 2:24). Leaving one's family involves more than a geographic journey, though sometimes this occurs as it did with Wesley. It principally involves a psychological and emotional journey of self-discovery and individuation. In it one has the opportunity to sift through relics and traditions from one's family of origin, deciding which to keep or modify and which to discard. No wonder family therapists insist one must leave home, individuate, and become a person

34. Baker, *Church of England*, 49–50.
35. Ibid.

more fully responsible for oneself in order to prepare to become a suitable marital partner.[36] The physical distance (and developing emotional distance) from England and family ties might have permitted Wesley the space to contemplate romantic attachments.

The full significance of journey for one's individuation and self-autonomy became crystal clear to me a few years ago. I attended a psychological seminar conducted by Jeffrey Kottler. In the seminar, Kottler told about a woman, symbiotically dependent on her husband. They journeyed together on a train somewhere in Europe. During the trip, the train stopped and the woman, still regaled in her sleeping outfit and robe, left the train to find a restroom. During her absence, the train left. On discovering this, she initially felt hopelessly lost and wondered how she would reach their original destination. But, desperate circumstances create desperate measures! Looking across the tracks, she saw another train pointed in the same general direction. She somehow boarded it and when it finally stopped, she again looked across the tracks and saw the original train from which she had disembarked. Making her way to it, she boarded it, found her way back to her compartment, and got into bed. Her husband had remained asleep during her absence and did not even know she had been gone. Given her recent experience in autonomy and self-direction, she was never as dependent again as she had been before. She became a much more independent woman, more confident, more assured in her abilities and her capacity to make trustworthy decisions. She did not pursue therapy to help her in these tasks, rather, she experienced a journey of individuation and it changed her.[37]

Journeying can create individuation and self-determination. In some measure, I think John Wesley's journey to Georgia and the time spent there similarly impacted him. I think Wesley needed Georgia to begin detachment from past family legacies, including the ecclesial, theological, and marital. Georgia provided an occasion to strip away, even, if not in their entirety, some of the vestiges of family legacies. Geographic distance from England also likely brought into view his relationship with the many women in his life—his mother, his sisters, and other female acquaintances. It provided him an opportunity to view another woman in a different light apart from these significant women in his life. Moreover, such distance would allow formation of a new identity without the influence of family

36. Carter and McGoldrick, *Family Life Cycle.*

37. Kottler, *Good, Bad and Ugly.*

ties. One should remember some of Wesley's family ties had already been broken. His father, Samuel Wesley, had died in June of 1735.[38] About four months later, on October 14, 1735, the Wesleys would embark for America (although they did not actually start the trip until December).[39] However, some suggest Wesley's trip to Georgia served to fulfill his father's dream.[40] In fact, one author described the mission as doing penance on a grand scale. The author indicated similar penance in Wesley in relation to his father on two other occasions: following his sermons against his father in the Hetty Wesley affair; and following his initial refusal to take over from his father at Epworth (although he would later accept the invitation, but by this time the appointment had been given to another).[41] Although this could be the case, I also think the death of his father provided an opportunity to become his own person, best done in another place.

Going to Georgia also permitted distance from his mother's and others' influence in his life. As I have indicated earlier, some authors speak about the dependence of the Wesley children on Susanna. This was also true for John Wesley, and some have suggested he was especially close to his mother.[42] Thus, with his mother a continent away, Wesley had more freedom to fully develop his own autonomy. Moreover, by the time he embarked for Georgia, many of Wesley's obligations to help support his family had ended, even if temporarily. His mother, Susanna, had moved in with Westley and Martha Hall and would later move to her son's, Samuel's, house.[43] Most of his sisters were ensconced in marriages or provided for in some other fashion. In fact, within two months of his boarding the ship for America, two of his three single sisters had married; Martha married Westley Hall in September 1735, and Emilia married Richard Harper the following month, a ceremony performed by John himself. Only Kezia remained unmarried and, although it appeared a problematic arrangement, like her mother, Susanna, she, too, had moved in with Wesley and Martha Hall. These arrangements freed the three brothers from the major responsibilities of providing for their sisters. One sister, Sukey (Susanna), continued to experience great difficulties in her marriage, and to ad-

38. Clarke, *Memoirs*; Ethridge, *Strange Fires*.

39. Tyerman, *Life and Times*.

40. Heitzenrater, *Elusive*; Moore, *Authority*.

41. Moore, *Authority*.

42. Green, *The Young*; Moore, *Authority*.

43. Rogal, *Susanna Annesley Wesley*.

dress this, John had apparently considered taking her and her children to Georgia, although this did not occur.[44] As a result, for perhaps the first time in his adult life, John was relatively free from the demands of his family and could pursue his journey without a great deal of distractions. Though Charles accompanied John on this journey, he resided in Savannah; Charles chiefly resided at Frederica. Such circumstances would likely further the process of individuation in John and open the possibility for pursuing an intimate relationship with Sophy Hopkey.

Rebound and Marriage: The Replication of a Tragic Family Pattern

I have chosen to devote the remainder of this chapter to relating the family's marriage patterns to John's marriage to Mary Vazeille. However, as a backdrop to this relationship, it is important to consider his relationship with Grace Murray. I do so because his marriage to Mary Vazeille appears to represent a rebound from his relationship with Grace Murray.[45] More importantly, the family marriage patterns evident in the unhappy marriages, and discussed in the previous chapter, appear most visibly and pronounced when one considers these two relationships together. In the earlier chapter, I suggested these patterns revolved around enmeshment, physical and emotional cutoff, and interference. I have incorporated these elements into a step-by-step process laid out below, and will mostly discuss them in this fashion. However, I have provided this linear process primarily for convenience. Rarely do such events follow these steps in strict sequential fashion. Rather, such relational events typically involve much more overlap and intermingling of the steps. Because of the difficulty capturing this more circular process, I have laid them out in this manner. Nevertheless, the steps serve to capture my understanding of the process, which exhibited itself in the unhappy relationships in the Wesley family:

Wesley Family Patterns in Unhappy Relationships

1. Enmeshment between members encouraged too much responsibility for each other in the context of intimate relationships. This is especially evident in the males in the family though not exclusively.

44. Maser, *Story of John Wesley's Sisters.*
45. Baker, "Wesley's First Marriage."

2. One or more family members become triangulated in the intimate relationship of another member and begin to actively interfere in the relationship.

3. The intimate relationship is usually disrupted and ends, leading to grief and disappointment at the loss.

4. The relationship's loss leads to some sense of emotional reactivity eventuating in a new relationship (the rebound effect)

5. To protect the new relationship, the member who experienced the loss either keeps it secret or does not consult or seek permission. This was sometimes facilitated by the physical and/or emotional cutoff, which occurred between family members following the interference.

6. The member solidifies the new relationship, most often in marriage, and the latter turns out disastrously.

The pattern outlined here appears quite consistently in the relationships of John Wesley's sisters. The interested reader can consult Frederick Maser's *The Story of John Wesley's Sisters: Seven Sisters in Search of Love*. A perusal of their stories would largely support the pattern I suggest here. But the most significant application of this pattern involves its connection to John Wesley and his intimate relationships. The astute reader, who possesses some information on Wesley's relationships with Grace Murray and Mary Vazeille, might recognize this pattern in these relationships.

One can assert, with some certainty, the existence of enmeshment between John and Charles Wesley. I have referred to their extreme closeness in earlier chapters. This closeness might even have influenced John's relationship with Grace Murray in the first place. John might have sought an intimate relationship because of the change in his bond with Charles due to the latter's marriage to Sarah Gwynne. Pursuing an intimate relation would allow him to replace, to some degree, the relationship that existed with his brother. Significantly, the formation of John's relationship with Grace Murray came a few months after Charles' marriage.[46] This same closeness and sense of responsibility for the other likely made Charles assume too much responsibility for John's intimate relationships with Grace Murray. Moreover, Charles' anxiety likely became heightened because he perceived John as ill suited for marriage. Given these concerns, coupled with Charles' apprehension about the fledgling Methodist movement, he

46. Lloyd, *Charles Wesley*.

became triangulated in John's relationship with Grace. Actually he did more; in a rather hasty and impulsive fashion, he quickly married her off to John Bennet.[47] Charles has received some notoriety for interfering in John's intimate alliance with Grace, but as disastrous as his action was, it was not unusual. Rather, it conforms well to the relationship patterns in the Wesley family, especially to the active interference by males undertaken to disrupt liaisons they considered ill advised.

In line with the pattern outlined previously, John's relationship came to a screeching halt. Charles' behavior in marrying off, to another man, a woman John considered his wife unearthed deep distress and hurt in the latter.[48] In fact, John's emotional response betrayed characteristics similar to those exhibited when he lost Sophy Hopkey to William Williamson. As before, he fell into a "slough of despond," indulging in searching introspection in the process. All the while, he denounced the effects of inordinate affection.[49] Although previously quoted, his entry of Sunday, October 1 bears repeating. On this occasion, Wesley wrote:

> I was in great heaviness, my heart was sinking in me like a stone. Only so long as I was preaching I felt ease. When I had done, the weight returned. I went to Church sorrowful and very heavy, though I knew not any particular cause. And God found me there[50]

Besides the hurt engendered in John, the Grace Murray affair contributed to estrangement between the brothers. In fact, Charles' behavior did lasting damage to their relationship.[51] Here, too, we see another characteristic evident in the Wesley family—emotional and physical cutoff. This phenomenon clearly appears in the words, which Charles spoke to his brother John in the aftermath of the disastrous event. This event was captured in John Wesley's journal entry for October 5, 1749, "About eight one came in from Newcastle, and told us, 'They were married on Tuesday.' My brother came an hour after. I felt no anger, yet I did not desire to see him. But Mr. Whitefield constrained me. After a few words had passed, he accosted me with, '*I renounce all intercourse with you, but what I would*

47. Baker, "Wesley's First Marriage"; Baker, "Some Observations"; Curnock, "The Journal"; Dobree, *Biography*; Rack, *Reasonable Enthusiast*.

48. Collins, *A Real Christian*; Curnock, "The Journal"; Ward and Heitzenrater, *The Works*, Vol. 18.

49. Curnock, "The Journal."

50. Curnock, "The Journal," Vol. 3, 435.

51. Lloyd, *Charles Wesley*.

have with an heathen or a publican"[52] (emphasis mine). These emphasized words from Charles represent a classic statement of emotional and, in this case, physical cutoff.

The loss of the relationship with Grace Murray dealt John a significant blow. Through Charles' one masterstroke, John lost a relationship he evidently cherished. At the same time, Charles's action left the brothers' relationship in tatters. Indeed, Charles had been like another self to John. Such significant losses—two with one blow—created an apparent emotional vacuum in John from which he attempted recovery through a hastily formed relationship with Mary Vazeille about a year and a half later. The eminent Wesley scholar, Frank Baker, even described the relationship with Mary Vazeille as a rebound from Grace Murray stimulated by his grief over his previous loss.[53] Given his previous vacillation in his relationships with Sophy Hopkey and Grace Murray, the haste with which Wesley moved in contracting a marriage with Mary Vazeille catches one by surprise. His action suggests some hint of desperation as captured by one author, "Whereas earlier John Wesley had been hesitating and cautious in the Hopkey and Murray affairs, now he was quick, bold and determined (some might even argue reckless), perhaps unwilling to be frustrated yet again."[54]

In addition to the tragic loss of Grace Murray, perhaps yet another family dynamic might have contributed to John's apparent desperation. By the time Charles married, all the Wesley siblings, with the exception of Kezia, had married. Whatever the reason, by 1749 John Wesley now felt a strong urge to marry. In his journal entry for February 2, 1751, Wesley wrote:

> *Sat.* 2. Having received a full answer from Mr. P——, I was clearly convinced that I ought to marry. For many years I remained single, because I believed I could be more useful in a single, than in a married state. And I praise God, who enabled me so to do. I now as fully believed, that in my present circumstances, I might be more useful in a married state; into which, upon this clear conviction, and by the advice of my friends, I entered a few days after."[55]

52. Curnock, "The Journal," Vol. 3, 439.
53. Baker, "John Wesley's First Marriage."
54. Collins, "John Wesley's Relationship," 8.
55. Ward and Heitzenrater, *The Works*, Vol. 20, 377–78.

Significantly, as in the case with both Sophy Hopkey and Grace Murray, a period of convalescence provided John the opportunity to cultivate his relationship with Mary, culminating in an actual proposal and a completed marriage.[56] However, in this case, John chose not to consult Charles or the Methodist societies prior to the marriage. Previously, John had resisted Grace Murray's urgings for marriage, because he did not think he could formalize a marriage with her until he had consulted both with Charles and the Methodist societies and gained their blessings. John and Charles had made a mutual agreement to consult each other prior to marriage when John returned from Georgia. Based upon this agreement, Charles consulted with John prior to his marriage to Sarah Gwynne.[57] Besides this, John himself, made consulting with the societies a rule to guide his ordained and lay preachers. Wesley advised his preachers they should not take any steps towards marriage until they had consulted their brothers.[58] But in the case of his marriage to Mary Vazeille, John violated both rules. In his journal entry for Saturday, February 2, 1751, John made reference to having consulted with Mr. Perronet. Wesley also referred to gaining the advice of his friends, although the identity of these friends remains a mystery.[59]

John Wesley in his Fortieth Year. A painting by Richard Douglas at Asbury Theological Seminary. Used with permission.

56. Baker, "John Wesley's First Marriage."

57. Wesley, C., *The Journal*, Vol. 2.

58. Collins, "John Wesley's Relationship"; *A Real Christian*; Rogal, "Wesley Takes a Wife."

59. Ward and Heitzenrater, *The Works*, Vol. 20.

One can easily understand why John Wesley did not consult Charles. After all, Charles served as the key player in marrying off Grace Murray to John Bennet. Charles would have no further opportunity to disrupt another relationship. Besides, the brother's relationship had been greatly disrupted by the Grace Murray affair. Charles had even reactively announced a cutoff in his relationship with his brother. In fact, the relationship continued at rather low ebb: John still remained in the throes of the hurtful repercussions stemming from his brother's impulsive action. Charles likely harbored residual anger as well as newly minted resentment because of John's behavior in the societies.[60] Besides their estrangement and differences over the societies, circumstances in Charles' life detracted from him serving as a good consultant to John. Apparently, at the beginning of 1751, Charles' own family affairs gave him cause for concern. Coincidentally, Charles' family problems mirrored the ongoing issues in the Wesley family; Charles' wife seemed as enmeshed with her siblings as was often true in the Wesley family and he appeared to experience great difficulty separating her from her sisters Betsy and Peggy.[61] One must wonder if the enmeshment evident between his wife and her sisters reminded Charles of his own enmeshment with his brother, John. Such a realization would likely make Charles more ready to break his dependency on his brother. Charles possessed some drastic, and not so healthy, options for breaking his almost symbiotic connection to his brother. He could self-differentiate from his brother through physically distancing, or he could do so emotionally through criticism of his brother. Charles apparently chose both. We have already referred to the physical estrangement between Charles and John, but Charles also demonstrated a critical frame of mind in his diary entries during this period. Charles criticized John's autocratic nature and unquestioned autocratic rule in the societies. He went so far as to criticize his brother in a public speech at the Foundery, even directing censure at the society.[62]

Given these circumstances, who could blame John for not consulting Charles? And consult he did not. As is indicated in a previous quotation from Charles' journal for February 2, 1751, he became dumbfounded when John told him he had resolved to marry. Later, Ned Perronet revealed the identity of the future Mrs. Wesley as Mary Vazeille. Charles had evidently

60. Ibid.
61. Curnock, "The Journal."
62. Ibid.

never entertained any idea Mrs. Vazeille could be his brother's intended. This grave news so shocked him, he distanced from his brother, refusing his company to the chapel. Instead, he retreated with his wife Sally to groan and grieve for several days about his brother's disastrous marriage. What's more, a deeply distraught Charles literally became incapacitated for a while, finding it difficult to eat, preach, or rest.[63] Given this entry, it appears clear Charles did not know the identity of the person whom John intended to marry. As I indicated elsewhere, Charles had previously met Mrs. Vazeille and considered her "a woman of a sorrowful spirit." He likely would not have approved of her as a suitable mate for his brother or the marriage a potentially happy one. On Sunday February 17th. 1751, Charles would hear John's apology at the Foundery. Several days after this, he described himself as one of the last ones to hear of his brother's ". . . unhappy marriage."[64]

The relationship between Charles and John and the latter's new mate would remain somewhat rocky, although both sides made attempts at reconciliation. Charles also helped the couple individually and together when the first signs of trouble began to appear in the relationship in June of 1751.[65] Coincidentally or not, John became so ill during this early period of his marriage, he thought he would die. Convinced of his impending demise, he wrote the epitaph for his tombstone.[66] John also sought full reconciliation between his brother and sister-in-law, as indicated by an entry from Charles' journal. In this entry, Charles noted John's request that they put their old grievances behind them. Charles readily agreed to this, offering Mrs. Wesley his service with sincerity. However, Charles seemed to hedge his bets to some degree as he added he would not suspect Mrs. Wesley, but hoped ". . . she will *do as she says.*"[67] Although one cannot fault John for failing to consult Charles about his impending marriage, this failure clearly fits the family's relational pattern. As I described earlier, following family interference in previous relationships, the Wesleys tended to keep future relationships secret or did not consult about them with family members. By keeping Charles in the dark about the identity of his intended marriage partner, John likely sought to

63. Wesley, C., *The Journal*, Vol. 2.
64. Ibid. 79.
65. Ibid.
66. Curnock, "The Journal."
67. Wesley, C., *The Journal*, Vol. 2, 97.

forestall any further interference and the disruption of this relationship, as had occurred with Grace Murray. What's more, the circumstances in Charles' life and his blatant critical attitudes towards John would have further dissuaded John from making further revelations about his marital intentions. Moreover, since he had spoken broadly to Charles about his resolve to marry, John could conceivably have argued he had fulfilled his arrangement with Charles.

Unfortunately, within the family, relationships created on the rebound and kept secret usually experienced great tumult and difficulties. This same family pattern, seen in the unhappy marriages in the Wesley family, held true in John's relationship with Mary Vazeille. Cracks quickly appeared in the relationship. Judging from Charles' accounts, small fissures began to appear as soon as June 1751. For example, on Friday, June 21, 1751, Charles wrote, "I found my sister in tears; professed my love, pity, and desire to help her. I heard her complaints of my brother, carried her to my house, where, after supper, she resumed the subject, and went away comforted."[68]

The next day, Charles wrote, "Sat. June 22d. I passed another hour with her, in free, affectionate conference; then with my brother; and then with both together. Our explanation ended in prayer and perfect peace."[69]

Kenneth Collins has written an excellent article in which he highlighted the tumultuous terrain of this relationship. He divided John Wesley's relationship with Mary Vazeille into the following four periods, which merit some discussion:

1. June 1750–April 1752 (Inordinate affection, and the work of the Lord)
2. May 1752–August 1764 (distrust, Jealousy, and Purloined Letters)
3. September 1764 to August 1774 (The growing rift)
4. September 1774 to October 1781 (Final Departure)[70]

Even though John Wesley married Mary Vazeille, he continued to betray a perspective of marriage, which considered it a form of inordinate affection when compared to the work of the Lord. For Wesley, love and marriage to a woman paled in comparison to love and service for God. In fact, it represented an irrational and unjustifiable relationship when

68. Ibid., 83.
69. Ibid.
70. Collins, "John Wesley's Relationship."

juxtaposed to the service of God. Moreover, for Wesley, marriage seemed a major obstacle to serving God.[71] Given this perspective on marriage and its relationship to ministry, one wonders why Wesley would even consider, let alone complete, a marital arrangement. He must have thought marriage would bring some benefit to ministry. In his case, it would put an end to aspersions cast upon him for being single, and the endless rumors that spiraled around him.[72]

Given Wesley's beliefs about the relationship of conjugal and ministry commitments, one could describe him as conforming to a sect-type clergy pattern. In this pattern, the minister capitulates to the demands of ministry without due attention to the needs of the marriage or family.[73] Earlier, Wesley had betrayed this perspective in his relationship with Sophy Hopkey. He evidently hesitated proposing to her, because it would have derailed his mission to the Indians. This was compounded by his belief in his lack of ability to endure the married state.[74] At that time, Wesley also perceived himself as being caught between affection for Sophy and his duty to God, with the former constituting inordinate affection.[75] No wonder Wesley provided a rather detailed analysis of inordinate affection in his account of the affair with Miss Sophy.[76]

We see similar sentiments in Wesley, even when it came to Grace Murray. Having concluded and confirmed Grace Murray as his intended, Wesley still placed the major emphasis on her usefulness as a partner in the gospel. Wesley wrote:

14. As to the latter, I have the strongest assurance, which the nature of the thing will allow, that *the person proposed would not hinder, but exceedingly further me in the work of the Gospel.* For, from a close observation of several years (three of which she spent under my roof) I am persuaded she is in every capacity an help meet for me.

15. First as a housekeeper. . . .

16. As a nurse. . . .

---

71. Ibid.

72. Telford, *The Life of John Wesley.*

73. Scanzoni, "Occupational-Conjugal Role Conflict."

74. Curnock, "The Journal"; Ward & Heitzenrater, *The Works*, Vol. 20.

75. Curnock, "The Journal."

76. Collins, "John Wesley's Relationship"; Curnock, "The Journal."

17. As a companion. . . .

18. As a friend. . . .

19. Lastly, *as a fellow labourer in the Gospel of Christ (the light wherein my wife is to be chiefly considered)* . . .[77] (Emphasis mine)

At least two emphases appear in his rationale. First, Wesley clearly considered Grace the most appropriate partner because of her usefulness in ministry. The first statement highlighted makes this abundantly clear. Wesley reinforced the idea in the last highlighted statement; he considered Grace's usefulness as a fellow servant in the gospel, the most compelling reason for marrying her. Even items 15–19 in Wesley's statement smacks of a utilitarian slant. Usefulness reigned supreme! Although Wesley loved Grace, he loved God and his work more. This utilitarian stance also influenced his marriage to Mary Vazeille. In his statement made on February 2, 1751 concerning his reasons for marriage, Wesley again struck a utilitarian chord. According to him, he had chosen to remain single for many years because he thought he could be more useful in this state. Likewise, he now thought he would be more useful in a married state. For Wesley, his primary concern seemed always to revolve around what would best serve ministry. If singleness, then so be it! If marriage, then he would marry! A few days later on February 6, 1751, he admonished the single men to remain single for the kingdom of heaven's sake.[78] At first glance, this statement seems inconsistent for a man who had recently decided to marry. On further consideration, it appears quite consistent; for John would stay single or marry depending upon which state best served and enhanced his ministry. Given this stance, Wesley would not allow marriage to restrict his call. One month following his marriage, he expressed how incomprehensible he considered it for a Methodist preacher to answer to God for preaching one less sermon or traveling one less mile in a married rather than in a single state.[79] Indeed, John Wesley reputedly told one Henry Moore that he and Mrs. Wesley had made such a pact— he would not preach one sermon or travel one less mile because of the

---

77. Heitzenrater, *Elusive*, 182.

78. Curnock, "The Journal."

79. Curnock, "The Journal"; Heitzenrater, *Elusive*; Rogal, "Wesley Takes a Wife"; Telford, *The Life of John Wesley*.

marriage. In fact, he noted, "If I thought that I should, my dear, as well as I love you, I would never see your face more."[80]

Given these views, no wonder trouble quickly appeared in his marriage. As stated earlier, as soon as June 1751, difficulties began to appear in the marriage, prompting Charles' involvement.[81] To her credit, Mary Wesley tried to accommodate her husband. Two weeks after her marriage, she traveled with him on a northern journey as well as to Cornwall. In fact, she traveled with him extensively during the first four years of the marriage.[82] Though she accommodated the early travels, problems yet existed for which many cast aspersions at her. For example, the Vicar of Shoreham accused her of harboring bitterness for many months and labeled her as possessing a bitter and an angry spirit.[83]

Kenneth Collins[84] characterized the second period of John Wesley's marriage as one of "distrust, jealousy, and purloined letters." This labeling seems most appropriate since John's letters to various women helped spawn Mary's jealous rage. She habitually read his letters, which he wrote to Sarah Ryan, Sarah Crosby, and others. In fairness to Mary, John gave her permission to open his letters, but driven by jealousy, she sometimes searched his pockets for letters. Some of these letters, though spiritual in nature and purpose, used language one normally reserves for intimate relationships such as marriage.[85] One such letter occasioned her first separation from John. The letter in question was one written by John to Sarah Ryan on January 20, 1758. I share a portion of this letter below:

> Most of the trials you have lately met with have been of another kind; but it is expedient for you to go through both evil and good report. The conversing with you, either by speaking or writing, is an unspeakable blessing to me. I cannot think of you without thinking of God. Others often lead me to him; but it is, as it were, going round about; you bring me straight into His presence. Therefore, whoever warns me against trusting you, I cannot

---

80. Telford, *The Life of John Wesley*, 254.

81. Telford, *The Life of John Wesley*; Wesley, C., *The Journal*.

82. Collins, "John Wesley's Relationship"; Telford, *The Life of John Wesley*.

83. Telford, *The Life of John Wesley*.

84. Collins, "John Wesley's Relationship."

85. Ibid.

refrain; as I am clearly convinced He calls me to it." "I am, Your affectionate brother."[86]

The letter so incensed Mary Wesley she separated from him that same day, but only for two days. We know the association of these events because of another letter John Wesley wrote to Sarah Ryan a week later:

MY DEAR SISTER,

January 27, 1758. LAST Friday, after many severe words, my —— left me, vowing she would see me no more. As I had wrote to you the same morning, I began to reason with myself, till I almost doubted whether I had done well in writing, or whether I ought to write to you at all. After prayer that doubt was taken away. Yet I was almost sorry that I had written that morning. In the evening, while I was preaching at the chapel, she came into the chamber where I had left my clothes, searched my pockets, and found the letter there, which I had finished, but had not sealed. While she read it, God broke her heart; and I afterwards found her in such a temper, as I have not seen her in for several years. She has contin- ued in the same ever since. So I think God has given a sufficient answer, with regard to our writing to each other.

I still feel some fear concerning you. How have you found yourself since we parted? Have you suffered no loss by anything? Has nothing damped the vigour of your spirit? Is honor a blessing, and dishonor too? the frowns and smiles of men? Are you one and the same in ease or pain; always attentive to the voice of God? What kind of humility do you feel? What have you to humble you, if you have no sin? Are you wise in the manner of spending your time? Do you employ it all, not only well, but as well as it is pos- sible? What time have you for reading? I want you to live like an angel here below; or rather, like the Son of God. Woman, walk thou as Christ walked; then you cannot but love and pray for Your affectionate brother."[87]

But other letters on different occasions also inspired jealousy in Mary Wesley. For example, she reacted similarly to letters to Sarah Crosby. Furthermore, she spoke evil of Wesley even to her domestic help, suggest- ing dalliances with various women.[88] Given her intense jealousies, one must wonder why John continued his correspondence with these women.

86. Telford, *The Letters,* Vol. 4, 4.

87. Jackson, "The Works," Vol. 12, 220-21.

88. Collins, "John Wesley's Relationship."

His very words written to Sarah Ryan in the letter of January 27, 1758, questioned the wisdom of such action. Yet, he claimed these doubts dissipated after prayer, a dubious conclusion given the negative impact on his marriage. Wesley evidently saw his letter writing as part of his spiritual ministry to these women. Given the preeminent focus of ministry in his life, even above his marriage, Wesley could faultily engage in their continuance, even though they contributed irreparable harm in his marriage. Baptizing his rationale through perceived confirmations from prayer would further solidify his resolution.

One might consider Wesley's correspondence with these women in another light; the correspondence could also have served as a form of triangulation. From this perspective, John Wesley sometimes triangulated these women into his marriage issues through his correspondence with them. As I indicated earlier, triangulation serves to diffuse anxiety in a dyadic relationship through bringing another into the relationship. Given the constant uneasiness in Wesley's marriage (even before the purloined letters), this conclusion seems plausible. The relationships with these women likely provided Wesley a more pleasant, though innocent relationship with a female than that experienced with his wife. He might also have used these relationships as an opportunity to vent about his difficulties at home.

In his review of the correspondence between John and Mary Wesley, Collins[89] demonstrated a period during 1764–1768 in which healing and possible resolution of their marital conflicts appeared achievable. But here again, Wesley's primary allegiance to ministry above his marriage raised its ugly head and contributed to another separation. Apparently, the critical event provoking Mary's departure was John Wesley's misguided ministry commitment above concern for his wife's health. Mary, evidently, had been ill, suffering from a fever. John visited her at the Foundery but remained for one hour to ensure her fever was broken. Once determined, Wesley continued his ministry trip to Bristol. As one could well understand, this perceived slight and callousness for her condition deeply affected Mary. Once recovered, she left Wesley.[90]

Finally, Collins[91] characterized the period from September 1774 to October 1781 as "The Final Departure." Mary left for good at the beginning

89. Ibid.
90. Ibid.
91. Ibid.

of this period. Again, as indicated by Wesley's conditions for her return, his correspondence with women played a critical role. According to Collins, Wesley required her to return his papers and promise not to take any more. Furthermore, he demanded she retract statements, which connected him to various women. I agree with the conclusions, which Kenneth Collins drew relative to the problems in Wesley's marriage. Although acknowledging the problems caused by Mary's reading of John's letters, Collins placed much of the blame on Wesley. Furthermore, Collins rightly highlighted how neglect of his wife, concomitant with correspondence with various women, could fuel suspicion in her mind relative to the nature of these relationships.[92]

Wesley's attitude towards marriage in relation to ministry didn't help his family problems. According to the language used by John Scanzoni,[93] Wesley utilized a sect-type approach when resolving conjugal and ministry tensions. According to this model, ministry responsibilities carried much more importance than marital obligations. Ministry should brook no rivals, even that of one's spouse. No wonder Wesley could leave so soon for his ministry tour to Bristol without much ongoing attention to his wife's recovery. Besides this misguided commitment to ministry, According to Kenneth Collins, Wesley betrayed a meticulous concern for time and its use. Together, these would make him appear callous to his wife. In addition, he too quickly and easily ignored his own contributions, laying the major fault at Mary's door.[94] Collins also referenced a dictatorial style, which demanded absolute obedience from his wife. These all contributed mightily to the breakdown of his marriage.[95]

Even here, I wonder whether one might trace the influence of family, especially the influence of his father's attitude and behaviors relative to ministry and marriage. I do not think it incorrect to suggest Samuel Wesley devoted such attention to ministry as to be neglectful of his family. Emilia Wesley captured some of this neglect. In April 1725, she wrote these previously quoted words to John Wesleys:

> ... but after we were gotten into our house and all the family were settled, in about a year's time, I began to find out we were ruined, then came on London journeys, convocations of blessed memory,

92. Collins, "John Wesley's Relationship," *A Real Christian.*
93. Scanzoni, "Occupational-Conjugal Role Conflict."
94. Collins, "John Wesley's Relationship."
95. Ibid.

that for seven winters my father was at London and we at home in intolerable want and affliction, then I learnt what it was to seek money and bread seldom having any without such hardships in getting it.[96]

Besides his time at conventions, Samuel Wesley seems to have spent most of his time attending to matters of the parish and writing his vast commentary on the book of Job. One might also trace Samuel's influence in John's authoritarian approach to his marriage. According to Collins,[97] John espoused a perspective on marriage, which lauded spousal obedience and the subservience of a wife to her husband. Furthermore, he noted in John a preoccupation with authority and obedience. In short, Collins noted John's attempt to rule his wife similarly to the rule he exercised in his societies. To further complicate matters, Collins pointed to John's tendency to avoid communication with his wife and for blaming her for their difficulties, while proclaiming his own righteousness. In my opinion, John's demand for absolute obedience from his wife might harkens back to his father and the latter's expectations of Susanna. I trace this attitude to a poem Samuel wrote about Susanna:

> She graced my humble roof, and blest my life,
> Blest me by a far greater name than wife;
> *Yet still I bore an undisputed sway,*
> *Nor was't her task, but pleasure to obey;*
> Scarce thought, much less could act, what I denied.
> In our low house there was no room for pride;
> Nor need I e'er direct what still was right,
> She studied my convenience day and night.
> Nor did I for her care ungrateful prove,
> But only used my power to show my love;
> Whate'er she asked I gave without reproach or grudge,
> For still she reason asked, and I was judge.
> All my command, requests at her fair hands,
> And her requests to me were all commands:
> To other's thresholds rarely she'd incline,
> Her house her pleasure was, and she was mine;
> Rarely abroad, or never, but with me,
> Or when by pity call'd, or charity.[98] (italics mine)

96. Wesley E., "Letter to John Wesley," April 7, 1725.

97. Collins, "John Wesley's Relationship."

98. Clarke, *Memoirs*, 419.

Though Samuel tempered the poem with expression of care and deeds of love, it yet rings with the undisputed sway of a husband in his home. For Samuel, a wife's primary duty is to obey. One might remember the circumstance of Samuel's separation from Susanna. In essence, he demanded obedience exhibited by conformity of her beliefs about the king to his own. Without this obedience, he physically and emotionally cut off from her. Evidently, the apple does not fall far from the tree! This phrase rings true whether the concern is marriage, or ministry, or how the two will coexist harmoniously. At least this appears true in John Wesley's marriage and ministry. Mrs. Mary Wesley would die in 1781 at Camberwell without Wesley's immediate knowledge. He discovered she had died a few days later as indicated by a letter written October 14, 1781, "I came to London, and was informed that my wife died on Monday. This evening she was buried though I was not informed of it till a day or two after."[99] Given the tragic contours of their marriage, the end seems almost expected.

99. Telford, *The Life of John Wesley*, 260.

chapter 8

Lessons in Life and Ministry from the Life of John Wesley

Stories significantly shape identity. They partly determine identity, preferences, and behavior. A large part of our stories derives from our family of origin, which probably comprises the most influential system to which an individual can belong.[1] This powerful influence comes packaged in the various narratives created within our family environments. Among other things, these narratives include the family legacies handed down through generations and the relational patterns, which dominated those environments. Because of these influences, family stories inevitably impact our everyday life and the way we practice ministry. This way of thinking forms the crux of Edward Wimberly's book, *Recalling our Own Stories: Spiritual Renewal In Religious Caregivers*. In his book, Wimberly delved into the major role played by personal history, family of origin issues, and culture in shaping our stories. Moreover, according to Wimberly, our stories subsequently influence identity, relationships, and the thinking, feeling, and behavioral styles we bring to ministry. Because of this reality, effective ministry demands understanding of our own stories. Cultivating such understanding makes possible the development of a healthy identity. Furthermore, it facilitates more appropriate responses to our call, while making more effective ministry possible.[2] Without such understanding, we risk allowing various myths, gleaned from our personal history, to dominate the way we function in life and ministry. Those myths, or mistaken beliefs, often derive from our early recollections as well as other circumstances that attended our early lives. These include

1. McGoldrick et al., *Genograms*.
2. Wimberly, *Recalling Our Own Stories*.

elements such as birth order, our naming process, and the roles we played in the family.[3]

As discussed in previous chapters, these elements played a significant role in John Wesley's life. Earlier, I discussed the role of early recollections in Wesley's life, including the separation and reconciliation of his parents prior to his birth, which likely formed one of the most significant early recollections of his life. Indeed, Wesley hinted at the significance this event posed for his own biography, although he did not share the specific ways it influenced him. We can also point to his salvation from the Epworth fire as another significant early recollection. Birth order also played a vital role seeing that at a critical period within the Wesley family, John became a replacement child whose birth helped assuage the pain and grief over several lost sons. Significantly, the influence of the naming process also loomed large in Wesley's life for he bore the name "John" on behalf of his two dead brothers—John and John Benjamin. He also thought he carried the name "Benjamin" as a memorial to a third brother of that name. Because of these and other converging circumstances in the Epworth family, Wesley became a *special* and central figure in the Wesley clan. All these factors would play a significant role in the style Wesley brought to life and ministry.

Throughout this book, I have tried to uncover John Wesley's story through investigating family recollections and relational dynamics. In addition, I have, on occasion, implied how these dynamics influenced his life and ministry. Like all of us, Wesley's story contained both assets and vulnerabilities. Among other elements, his assets included his Anglican tradition, the dedication to learning and piety within the family, and love and service to the church.[4] Besides these, one can point to the influence, which must have proceeded from the long line of clergy in the Wesley and Annesley's lines. But Wesley's story also included a number of vulnerabilities, especially related to relational patterns in the family. These patterns included problems around individuation, family enmeshment and relational interference, and physical and emotional cutoff.

Contrary to the opinion held by some persons, God does not erase or negate the influence of one's background, assets, and vulnerabilities once we enter a relationship with him. Neither does our status as min-

---

3. Ibid.
4. Edwards, *Sons to Samuel*.

istry professionals erase these liabilities. Our relationship with God, or call by God, does not confer on us any godlike qualities or negate our personal history. Even after our salvation experience or call, clergy and other ministry professionals remain as human as the average person—liable to all the vicissitudes of mortality with its various vulnerabilities. Thus, to entertain thoughts about being redeemed or called as antidotes to human vulnerabilities represents an exercise in futility. Long after we have entered a relationship with God, long after we have been called, our stories influence the way we think, feel, and act in our daily lives as well as in ministry. I do not mean to suggest no moderation takes place because of our conversion or call, especially in relation to our vulnerabilities. Indeed, through varied means and relationships, and through our cooperation with grace, God continues to work with us at the point of our vulnerabilities. However, the possibility of overcoming some of the negative aspects of our vulnerabilities becomes more possible when one becomes aware of these tensions within us. With awareness comes the possibility of making responsible choices relative to grappling with our vulnerabilities. Without awareness, making responsible choices becomes nigh impossible.[5] For this reason, becoming aware of, and recalling, our stories looms large: These processes provide us a better chance of understanding them and then negating most of the negative impact on our lives and ministry.[6] In this final chapter, I wish to pull together the major points at which John Wesley's narrative influenced his life and ministry, and, in the process, touch on both strengths and vulnerabilities. By speaking about them somewhat separately, I do not mean to suggest they exist as separate spheres. Life and ministry never really diverge, even if we think they do; they remain inseparable parts of our being and functioning, deriving from our systemic makeup. Because of this artifact of our nature, life and ministry always mutually influence each other.

Lessons from John Wesley's Life

The Role of Early Environments in Habit Formation

From my perspective, John Wesley's narrative exerted profound influence on his life. I could speak about the impact on his personality, including his

5. Headley, *Created for Responsiility.*
6. Wimberly, *Recalling Our Own Stories.*

authoritarian stance, his ability to greatly influence others, and thereby extract deference from them.[7] However, I have chosen to largely focus on relational dynamics in Wesley's life. To a lesser extent, I will give some attention to the apparent drivenness, which seemed to characterize his life. As I have suggested in earlier chapters, Wesley's early environment, dominated by feminine relations, exerted primary influence in his personal narrative.[8] That early environment included his mother, seven sisters, and at least two nannies. This environment likely contributed to strengths and vulnerabilities in his life.

John Wesley's feminine environment contributed many positives to his life, shaping both his personality and his approach to life. In this regard, his mother, Susanna, exerted profound influence on John Wesley. She appears to have been the primary shaper of his personality and emotional life.[9] From her, he likely learned a consistently calm and unflappable approach to life.[10] Wesley exemplified this trait in much of his life. The exception appeared when he found himself deep in the throes of anguish and pain, usually apparent in the aftermath of the loss of intimate relationships. Besides this personality trait, one can likewise point to his strong rational approach, also gleaned from his mother. From her, John also "... inherited a studious, thoughtful disposition and a calm, stubborn patience under adversity . . ."[11] Susanna also exerted profound influence on John in terms of the development of his own spirituality, as well as his theological views and scholarship.[12] She often served as his confidante and the sounding board for the various theological questions he raised, and to which she responded. Some the letters she wrote to John offered her views on the Lord's afflictions and the nature of the presence of Christ in communion.[13] In other letters, she discussed her views on temptation, and, as well, agreed with John relative to his thoughts on various degrees of virtue and piety, and even with his opinion regarding William Law.[14] She even provided him counsel on whether his group (the Holy Club)

7. Abelove, *Evangelist of Desire*; Moore, *Authority*.

8. Abelove, *Evangelist of Desire*; Moore, *Authority*; Rack, *Reasonable Enthusiast*.

9. Rack, *Reasonable Enthusiast*.

10. Edwards, *Sons to Samuel*.

11. Baker, *Church of England*, 7.

12. Rogal, "Ladies Huntington, Glenorchy."

13. Wesley, Susanna, "Letter to John Wesley," 21 Feb. 1732.

14. Wesley, Susanna, "Letter to John Wesley," Jan 1 1734.

should discuss secular matters. In her opinion, such discussions held no problem unless they proved harmful.[15] Susanna took the opportunity to spice her responses to John with motherly advice relative to caring for his own self, while addressing his consumption.[16] Of course, Susanna also influenced John's views about education, sharing with him her approach for educating her children in a Christian manner.[17]

But his sisters likely also influenced him. Evidence from the family letters suggested his sisters evidently doted on him and often competed for his attention. They consistently sought him out and provided him with their own unique perspective on matters of the heart and life in general. In many respects, John Wesley became their counselor, a role, which he replicated with many other women in his ministry. Likely, their company and correspondence made him accustomed to, and comfortable with, the company of women, especially where the relationship was uncomplicated by romantic attachments. Of course, as we will see later, this latter issue also posed problems.

These influences and experiences likely shaped his attitudes and practices towards women in general. Wesley betrayed a contrasting attitude to the deeply entrenched patriarchy of his day, and went against the grain of established practice in many significant ways. Contrary to the practice in other religious societies, John welcomed women into his societies. Moreover, he encouraged their education.[18] This doubtlessly was influenced by the benefits he had seen in his own mother and sisters. Through his distinct habit of calling women "sister," one author suggested he narrowed the social distance, which existed between the men and women of his day.[19]

Besides these very positive influences, one can also point to vulnerabilities, which derived from his early environment. Rack[20] characterized this influence as the "feminization of Wesley." Rack saw this feminine environment, including Susanna's influence, contributing to Wesley's troubled relationships with women during his life. In similar fashion, Moore[21]

15. Wesley, Susanna, "Letter to John Wesley," 30 March, 1734.

16. Wesley, Susanna, "Photographic copy of a letter," 25 Oct, 1732.

17. Dallimore, *Susanna*; Wesley, Susanna, "Letter to John Wesley," 21 Feb. 1732.

18. English, "'Dear Sister.'"

19. Ibid.

20. Rack, *Reasonable Enthusiast*.

21. Moore, *Authority*.

noted how John Wesley's early experiences in the home contributed to his love for the company of women. According to him, such experiences provided John the possibility of intimacy untainted by passion or desire. Moore also highlighted Susanna's influence in John Wesley's intimate relationships. According to him, Susanna emphasized guarding against 'Delilah.' According to Moore, 'Delilah' was Susanna's personification of temptation to sinful willfulness. As a result, John learned to guard against fleshly passions and sexuality to a heightened degree. From his environment and these messages, Wesley likely developed his ambivalence towards intimate relationship. Though attracted to women, he characterized such associations as inordinate affect, especially when they competed with his devotion to ministry. This notion contributed to his hesitancy in intimate relationships. It created what Moore described as a "conflict between attraction and conscience." But, as I implied elsewhere, we can also explain his hesitancy and ambivalence in relationships by other means. For example, I doubt the number of conflicted marriages he saw in his family members would have made intimate relationships an attractive option. To further compound difficulties in these areas, John (as well as Charles), through no real fault of their own or their environment, shared a major problem: women found them attractive and naturally gravitated to them. As early as 1740, one John Hutton wrote the following comments to Count Zinzendorf about John and Charles Wesley, "The Wesleys are a snare to young women . . . all fall in love with them."[22]

Broadly speaking, the authors cited above largely highlighted two problems related to Wesley's early upbringing. First, they largely described how his early family constellation might have influenced his ambivalence and difficulties in intimate relationships with women. Because I have already discussed these relationships, I will not devote more attention to them here, although I will revisit them in order to discuss problems of dual relationships in pastoral ministry. Second, the authors described the degree of comfort with women, which his environment engendered (when not involving intimacy), and the creation of a craving for their company. Though one might characterize the first influence as negative, one cannot make the same judgment about the latter sphere of influence. Rather, whether this influence proved negative would largely depend on the individual's judgment and how he or she managed such relationships.

22. Edwards, *Astonishing Youth*, 49.

In Wesley's case, it did cause problems, but I do not think one can lay the results directly at the door of his early environment. Nevertheless, one can at least agree with the degree to which it might have contributed to a desire for the company, and for correspondence with women.

As mentioned in an earlier chapter, Wesley corresponded with women three times as much as he did with men, and continued this pattern unabated throughout his life.[23] In his defense, his correspondence with them possessed an innocent air and was designed to serve their spiritual welfare.[24] However, at times his letter struck an intimate tone, which best-befitted marital partners. Inevitably, this correspondence and the intimacy revealed therein, contributed to the breakdown of his marriage.[25] But even before his marriage to Mary Vazeille, Wesley had experienced complications and jealousies in his relationship with Grace Murray. Many of these complications were occasioned by rumors and gossip connecting John Wesley with other women, such as Molly Francis. On one occasion, rumors linking Wesley with the latter woman created such jealousy in Grace Murray, she renewed contact with John Bennet, a rival suitor for her hand.[26] This jealousy and resulting action no doubt stemmed from her anxiety regarding the permanence of her relationship with Wesley.

In addition, Wesley's close contact with women created other kinds of problems. Gossip and rumors about his relationships with women swirled around him. Some labeled him a bachelor rake, even prompting the Bishop of Exeter to accuse him of libertinism, because of his unmarried state. Newspaper stories would describe tete a tetes with various women,[27] and though innocent and intended for spiritual purposes, his familiarity with many women seemed to lend an air of credence to the distorted stories, contributing to charges of sexual misconduct.[28] In part, Wesley used this state of affairs as an argument for his proposed marriage to Grace Murray. He hoped marriage would put an end to the rumors about his supposed dalliances. Ironically, even his relationship with Grace Murray provoked rumors and jealous discussions in the Methodist societies, particularly

23. Edwards, *My Dear Sister.*
24. Edwards, *Astonishing Youth.*
25. Collins, "John Wesley's Relationship"; *A Real Christian.*
26. Baker, "John Wesley's First Marriage"; Maser, "Only Marriage."
27. Abelove, *Evangelist of Desire.*
28. Rack, *Reasonable Enthusiast.*

among females.[29] Even after he married Mary Vazeille, rumors persisted with his new bride joining in spreading these rumors.[30]

Given the difficulties his contact with women posed for his relationships, reputation, and Methodism's good name, one must wonder why Wesley persisted in such relationships. Given this immense cost, one would think Wesley would have restrained his correspondence and contact to some degree.[31] But persist he did! In my opinion, the most logical answer to explain this dangerous persistence revolves around the power of his feminine background and how it shaped his need for the company of females. His background held such emotional power over him, it outweighed concerns for his relationships, especially his marriage and his reputation. Furthermore, as we have seen, given the spiritual purposes intended by his correspondence, Wesley could easily dismiss the legitimate concerns raised by his wife, even while his behaviors did irreparable damage to his marriage. On the same grounds, Wesley could ignore the swirling rumors associating him with women at various times. All the while, his behavior helped to cast aspersions on him and his movement.

These examples demonstrate the power of our early environments to shape us profoundly. Our early environments, especially our family environment, can help develop within us deeply entrenched habits, which seem to operate by default, without conscious rational checks. These habits can be worthy, innocent, or damaging. Yet, whatever their nature, they can become deeply entrenched within us and exert such power so as to defy assessment and moderation, even when necessary. Indeed, these habits can overwhelm our capacity to reason objectively about their nature and impact in our lives, even when the negative consequences clearly appear to all. This appears true in Wesley's case. His need for female contact seems to have overpowered his ability to reason objectively about the disastrous results of such contact. Given this stance, his emotional need for contact with women defied logic and permitted the ignoring of objective evidence relative to their personal and ecclesial consequences. One might explain his persistent contact in another way; namely, Wesley engaged in reasoning, but not of the objective, rational sort. Instead he engaged in an emotional reasoning process, which he could easily confuse

29. Lloyd, *Charles Wesley*.

30. Abelove, *Evangelist of Desire*.

31. Rack, *Reasonable Enthusiast*.

with rational reasoning. As implied in an earlier chapter, this confusion indicates the presence of problems in self-differentiation. Specifically, it involves a problem in intrapsychic differentiation making distinguishing between emotional and intellectual processes difficult. In such cases, the individual becomes flooded with feelings making objective thinking nigh impossible.[32] We saw a prior and distinct example of this in John Wesley's relationship with Sophy Hopkey when they traveled from Frederica to Savannah. Though bent on pursuing singleness, but overcome with emotion from her prolonged presence, Wesley made an oblique proposal, uncensored by reason. His journal entry for February 3, 1737 demonstrates the conflict between reason and emotion.

> Feb. 3 I was now in a great strait. I still thought it best for me to live single. And this was still my design; but I felt the foundations of it shaken more and more every day. Insomuch that I again hinted at a desire of marriage, though I made no direct proposal. For indeed it was only a sudden thought which had not the consent of my own mind . . .[33] (italics mine)

The last sentence highlights his non-rational decision. Evidently, his proposal did not proceed from a rational decision, but from the throes of impulsive, emotion-driven "thought." His emotional turmoil and conflict would continue for several days. A few days later, Wesley would write:

> Tuesday 8 (Feb)—The next morning I was obliged to go down to Savannah. There I stayed about an hour; and there again I felt, and groaned under the weight of, an unholy desire. My heart was with Miss Sophy all the time. I longed to see her, were it but for a moment.[34]

To speak of this kind of emotional process, which defied reason in John Wesley, may seem a stretch for those who know him. After all, Wesley was known for his rational approach, his even temperedness, and his imperturbability.[35] How could one so rational be swayed by his emotions in intimate relationships? The answer may lie in a concept I call the pendulum principle. By this term, I mean one should expect radical shifts in an individual who betrays an extreme tendency. In this case, Wesley's

---

32. Nichols, *Family Therapy*; Skowron, "Differentiation of Self."

33. Curnock, "The Journal," Vol. 1, 315.

34. Ibid., 317.

35. Edwards, *Sons to Samuel*.

extreme rationality, under situations of intense conflict, could lead to an opposite extreme—in this case, an extreme emotional response. In such a rational individual who rarely allowed place for his feelings, his emotional makeup would become a kind of shadow side, waiting for an opportune moment to break out. Because it was rarely expressed, it would become an unconscious need, which would dominate those moments when it saw the light of day.

Before proceeding, it appears important to discuss his contact with women, because of its sensitive, critical nature and relevance for our times. I say this because of the prevalence of sexual misconduct in our day. This discussion is not meant to characterize Wesley's relationships as sexual misconduct, in our sense of the term. From my reading of many of his correspondences with women, Wesley clearly intended spiritual purposes. Nevertheless, the contacts created major problems in his life and ministry, and even produced misfounded allegations of wrongdoing. As in his case, clergy or other persons in ministry can become involved in varied and sometimes inappropriate relationships because of needs created from early experiences. Sometimes these needs go unmet, and thereby become sources of frustration. In the latter instances, these can become a source of problems for people in ministry, sometimes leading to charges and actual cases of sexual misconduct. In *Betrayal of Trust*, Stanley Grenz and Roy Bell[36] discussed three types of persons who become involved in sexual misconduct. In each case, the individual carried within them various unmet needs. First, Grenz and Bell discussed the *Predator*, one often motivated by unmet sexual and/or power needs, or who have unresolved personal problems. Second, they described the *Wanderer*, whom they characterized as a less successful person exuding inadequacy and vulnerability. For such persons, the satisfaction of private needs is played out in a public sphere and serves as an ill-conceived method of bolstering one's fragile sense of self. Moreover, wanderers become much more liable to engage in misconduct during stressful times occasioned by personal crises or transitions steeped in anxiety. Lastly, they described the *Lover* who is motivated by perceived love for a congregant. Although they know this to be love working out itself in a forbidden zone, they seem unable to temper their passions sufficiently to avoid the disastrous consequences.[37]

36. Grenz and Bell, *Betrayal of Trust*.
37. Ibid.

Given the power of our sometimes unconscious and unmet needs, the wise minister seeks to cultivate awareness and develops strategies to address these needs appropriately. This sometimes means one must avoid situations that tweak our needs and potentially tarnish our reputations or sully the name of Christ and the ministry.

Dual Relationships

Although I run the risk of inviting accusations of judging issues in Wesley's life from the perspective of present standards, I will now address dual relationships in his life and ministry. Clergy dual relationships represent situations in which a minister and a parishioner connect through additional roles including social, sexual, or business ones.[38] Given this definition, one can characterize Wesley's connections with Sophy Hopkey and Grace Murray as dual relationships. He evidently served as the pastoral figure for both women. Sophy clearly held membership in his flock at Savannah, Georgia, and Grace belonged to the society in Newcastle. But he would later become suitor to both. By falling in love with both and acting on such feelings, Wesley tried to simultaneously serve as pastoral leader and suitor. These contrasting roles would complicate life and interactions with both women, because of the difficulty involved in balancing them. How does one effectively balance the roles of pastoral leader and suitor to the same parishioner? Which of these roles takes precedence in interactions with the parishioner, and when? Such considerations make this an extremely difficult task to pull off. Moreover, such relationships rarely exist on equal footing, since the parties possess different levels of power—the pastoral leader always holds the upper hand, making an equal relationship almost impossible. If problems develop in such relationships (which they invariably do), extreme complications can result, with potential dire consequences for everyone associated with it. These complications can attend any phase of the relationship, including the beginning or the end. An investigation of these two relationships, which Wesley developed, will support the complications that can ensue when a pastoral leader becomes the suitor of a congregant.

In the case of Sophy Hopkey, one must wonder about her admiration and possible love for Wesley. Given the difference in age (Wesley being

38. Bleiberg and Skufca, "Clergy Dual Relationships"; Kane, "Sexual Misconduct."

almost twice her age) and the power of his position, one can understand the admiration and awe he must have struck in her. Furthermore, as noted by one author, besides looking up to Wesley, she both loved and feared him.[39] One can almost understand this admixture of emotion, given their differences. Indeed, Sophy seemed to have betrayed deference for Wesley, which led her to acquiesce to him in almost every matter. Wesley himself wrote the following words on January 31, 1737:

> . . . it was not her custom to deny me anything. For indeed from March 13, 1736, the day I first spoke to her, till that hour, I cannot recollect so much as a single instance of my proposing anything to her, or expressing any desire, which she did not comply with.[40]

Such deference might make one wonder whether love or reverential fear dominated Sophy's emotions in relation to John Wesley. The conflicting presence of these two emotions would seem to indicate the contradictions, which can exist in a parishioner caught in a dual relationship. For there exists both fear and awe towards the individual as pastoral leader, coupled with supposed love for the same person as suitor, all coexisting together in one confusing mass.

But beyond such concerns, tangible problems ensued when Sophy suddenly and surprisingly married William Williamson. Thereafter, her new marital status would lend a different perspective to Wesley's contact with her. In the opinion of some, legitimate pastoral oversight would now be tainted with the supposed stain of a jilted lover. Early on, William Williamson, biased by jealousy, would forbid Wesley from seeing his wife. But all hell would break loose when, on apparent principle and religious grounds, Wesley barred Sophy Williamson from communion. This event occurred on August 7, 1737. The very next day, the Williamsons would have a warrant drawn up against John Wesley, calling for his arrest. The warrant accused Wesley of defaming Sophy and refusing to publicly administer her holy communion, without due cause. William Williamson would claim damages of some one thousand pounds. The Caustons also became incensed by Sophy's disbarment and demanded satisfaction. Wesley became a frequent topic of conversation at the Causton's home, during which they reviled him with every evil name imaginable. Mr. Causton spread news in which he shared his ill-perceived perspectives on

39. Curnock, "The Journal."
40. Curnock, "The Journal," Vol. 1, 313–14.

Wesley's character. He even threatened to publish derogatory stories about John Wesley in every newspaper in England and America. The rest of the family joined in this barrage against Wesley to whoever would listen. They noted, "that Mr. Wesley had done this merely out of revenge, because Sophy would not have him."[41] These dire and humiliating circumstances would lead to John Wesley's ignominious escape from Georgia.

Similar complications occurred in Wesley's relationship with Grace Murray. As discussed earlier, Wesley's relationship with Grace Murray, the housekeeper at his Newcastle headquarters, created difficulties at a number of levels. It created differences with his brother Charles, who thought Grace too low bred and who argued a marriage to her would destroy the societies. Furthermore, following Charles brash action in marrying Grace off to John Bennet, an estrangement developed between the brothers, contributing to lasting damage in their relationship.[42] But John's relationship also created jealousies in the societies, especially among female members who might have entertained their own designs on John.[43] As one would expect, Wesley's relationship with Grace also created tensions between Wesley and the rival suitor for her hand, John Bennet, who had become one of Wesley's itinerant preachers in 1744.[44] Given their competing claims for Grace's hand, one would expect such tensions, especially since each had twice proposed and twice been accepted.[45] Accordingly, one of Wesley's desired actions before formally marrying Grace Murray was to set the matter straight with Bennet.[46] Following Bennet's marriage to Grace, John Bennet eventually disassociated himself from the Wesleyan Methodists. When he left, he split two Methodist societies and took 127 members from the Bolton society, leaving a mere nineteen. In Stockport, the society broke away from Wesley's movement to join Bennet, leaving but one woman.[47] Besides these unfortunate consequences to others and his movement, the abrupt end to his relationship with Grace caused John immense pain. The hurt appeared similar to that

41. Ward and Heitzenrater, *The Works*, Vol. 18, 543.

42. Curnock, "The Journal"; Lloyd, *Charles Wesley*.

43. Lloyd, *Charles Wesley*.

44. Tyerman, *Life and Times*.

45. Ward and Heitzenrater, *The Works*.

46. Baker, "Wesley's First Marriage"; "Some Observations."

47. Telford, *Life of John Wesley*.

which he displayed when he lost Sophy Hopkey. In the aftermath of his loss, Wesley wrote, "I was in great heaviness, my heart was sinking in me like a stone. Only so long as I was preaching I felt ease. When I had done, the weight returned. I went to Church sorrowful and very heavy, though I knew not any particular cause. And God found me there."[48] A few days following the wedding, John would write a letter to Thomas Bigg of Newcastle in which he poured out his disappointment. Though previously cited, it is worth repeating to underscore the significant damage this dual relationship created for John:

> Leeds, October 7th, 1749
>
> MY DEAR BROTHER,
>
> Since I was six years old, I never met with such a severe trial as for some days past. For ten years God has been preparing a fellow-labourer for me by a wonderful train of providences. Last year I was convinced of it; therefore I delayed not, but, as I thought, made all sure beyond a danger of disappointment. But we were soon torn asunder by a whirlwind. In a few months, the storm was over; I then used more precaution than before, and fondly told myself, that the day of evil would return no more. But it soon returned. The waves rose again since I came out of London. I fasted and prayed, and strove all I could; but the sons of Zeruiah were too hard for me. The whole world fought against me, but above all my own familiar friend. Then the word was fulfilled, "Son of man, behold, I take from thee the desire of thine eyes at a stroke; yet shalt thou not lament, neither shall thy tears run down."
>
> The fatal irrevocable stroke was struck on Tuesday last. Yesterday I saw my friend (that was), and him to whom she is sacrificed. I believe you never saw such a scene. But "why should a living man complain, a man for the punishment of his sins?"
>
> I am, yours affectionately,
> John Wesley[49]

The dual relationships with Sophy Hopkey and Grace Murray obviously caused a great degree of problems for John and all others systemically connected to him and them. This ought not to be surprising, but I suspect it is to some. Though not always, dual relationships typically create problems because of power imbalances and the difficulty managing

---

48. Curnock, "The Journal," Vol. 3, 435.
49. Telford, *Life of John Wesley*, 248–49.

the competing roles of minister and lover at the same time. Because of the problems and the ethical dilemmas, such relationships are roundly discouraged in the psychotherapeutic fields. Unfortunately, in my opinion, they receive less attention among persons in ministry, except when related to discussions of sexual misconduct. Indeed, as far as I know, there exists no professional code of conduct, which explicitly forbids dual relationships. As has been observed in some situations, church members might actively welcome a dating relationship and subsequent marriage between a single minister and a congregant.[50] Even in Wesley's case, this proved true. Sophy's uncle, Mr. Causton, implicitly invited the match between his niece and John.[51] But given the complications of such arrangements, these relationships ought to receive more attention and, possibly, specific ethical discouragement, across all denominations. Such relationships become too rife with complications and potential disaster, as Wesley's case amply demonstrates.

Before leaving this discussion of Wesley's relationship to women, it seems appropriate to briefly revisit the discussion of Wesley's resolution of tensions between his marriage and his ministry. I have already addressed how his correspondence with females created great tensions in his life. Here I wish to briefly review how Wesley resolved tensions between his marriage and his ministry. Elsewhere in this text, I suggested Wesley displayed a sect-type approach to ministry, giving preeminence and priority to ministry above his marriage. Coincidentally, this choice proved the final straw in the breakup of his marriage. On that occasion, though showing some concern for his wife's illness, after finding her somewhat improved, Wesley continued his ministry trek. For Mary, this was the final straw, which irrevocably broke down their marriage.[52] Though difficult to prove, I have little doubt such problems in resolving conjugal and ministry tensions partly flowed from observation of his father's devotion to ministry, sometimes above his family's wellbeing.

Wesley's Drivenness

Before delving more explicitly into the ministry consequences evident in Wesley's life, I wish to address an apparent personality trait. Here I

50. Bleiberg and Skufca, "Clergy Dual Relationships."

51. Curnock, "The Journal."

52. Collins, "John Wesley's Relationship."

speak of a drivenness, which seemed to characterize his life. John Wesley seemed a man on a mission, driven by a sense of special destiny. As I indicated in an earlier chapter, John did not necessarily see himself a child of special destiny and affirmed the same in a response to Mr. Badcock in 1784.[53] But, even with this rebuttal, it seems hard to miss the drivenness exhibited in his life and ministry. Whether Wesley consciously believed, thought, or advocated this perspective, his life yet exhibited drivenness, which often derives from the sense of being called to a special mission. From our earlier discussions, we can trace this trait to at least three early influences in his life: Wesley's salvation from the Epworth fire of 1709;[54] the specialness Susanna attributed to him and her subsequent desire to exert greater care for his soul and to instill true religion in him;[55] and his status as a replacement child. No wonder he demonstrated such purpose and resolve in his life! He was man on a mission, and nothing would stand in his way of accomplishing his purposes. Significantly, his drivenness and commitment, especially to ministry, fueled a kind of tunnel vision, where everything else paled in significance, even his intimate relationships, and his marriage.

Besides paying attention to such habits and traits fostered in childhood, individuals also need to guard against other patterns. I could discuss a variety of problems such as entitlement and specialness, and an inappropriate need for attention. However, I wish to address related habits, which Wimberly described as the myths of over-responsibility and self-sacrifice.[56] Both habits, in some sense, apply to Wesley. He exhibited extreme care and concern for others in all he did. He constantly catered to the spiritual, emotional, and physical needs of those under his care. At the same time, there appeared less concern for himself (given his hectic and demanding schedule) and, concomitantly, less concern for the intimate others in his life, especially his wife. In cases involving over-responsibility and self-sacrifice, persons who exhibit such tendencies usually took on the role of caregiver early in life. We cannot definitively place a family caregiver's role on Wesley, although his sisters seemed to look to him as their counselor and confidante. But, one can point to the sense of destiny and purpose gleaned from the circumstances of his birth and early life,

53. Heitzenrater, *Elusive*.
54. Curnock, "The Journal"; Heitzenrater, *Elusive*.
55. Telford, *Life of John Wesley*.
56. Wimberly, *Recalling Our Own Stories*.

as possibly instilling such patterns in him. However engendered, Wesley's life seemed devoted to others' wellbeing to such an extent, his own needs often seemed placed on hold. Even his desire for love and intimacy would be placed on hold to fulfill his purposes in ministry. But even when he married, the demands of ministry would yet hold sway in his life. As a result, Wesley made a pact with his wife not to travel one less mile or preach one less sermon. To drive home his point, Wesley told Mary, "If I thought that I should, my dear, as well as I love you, I would never see your face more.[57]" Furthermore, Wesley declared he could not understand how a Methodist could answer to God for preaching one less sermon or traveling one less mile in a married state than in a single.[58] This might have been a veiled slap at his brother Charles who had curtailed his travels after his marriage.[59] But even in the events surrounding his marriage, one yet saw another instance of Wesley ignoring his own needs. Prior to his marriage, Wesley had done severe damage to his ankle and had to be nursed by Mary Vazeille. Apparently, he still experienced problems with his foot after his marriage, but went right back to ministry before his foot healed. On February 19 and 20, 1751, Wesley preached from a kneeling position. A fortnight later he would set out to Bristol for a preachers' conference, barely able to ride[60] Evidently, this pattern became a deeply entrenched one in John's life.

This pattern can prove deeply troublesome in the life of a Christian minister. Because it springs to some degree from genuine concern for others, it can seem to possess a spiritual quality, even when done in an extreme way. Given this deeply ingrained habit, ministers can easily become oblivious of, and almost incapable of, attending to their own needs. They sometimes become rescuers, keenly attuned to the presence of needs or pain in others. All the while, they remain insensitive to pain in themselves.[61] This habit then exhibits itself in a number of different forms, but primarily shows itself in over-responsibility or self-sacrifice. In the first pattern, the individual develops a primary sense of responsibility for the needs and welfare of others. Concomitant with this, they exhibit under-responsibility for themselves and the intimate individuals in their lives,

57. Telford, *Life of John Wesley*, 254.

58. Ibid.

59. Tyerman, *Life and Times*, Vol. 2.

60. Heitzenrater, *Elusive*.

61. Steinke, *How Your Church Family Works*.

especially family. In the second related pattern, such persons devote themselves to sacrificing themselves for others, often with devastating personal consequences. It is a devastatingly dangerous pattern for one's personal life or one's functioning in ministry.

Given the power of early influences in our stories, it becomes important to gain awareness of, to recall, and investigate them. By so doing, we can maximize the strengths inherent in them. At the same time, we can seek to minimize the negative impact of the vulnerabilities deriving from our history. Unfortunately, those called to ministry often seem somewhat reluctant to take a serious and careful look at their own lives. As a result, they sometimes function with deeply gaping wounds and needs to which they remain unconscious. Sometimes these unconscious wounds and needs become unconscious motivators, seeping out furtively to cause all kinds of chaos in their lives and relationships. Often, only after disaster strikes or they hit bottom do such persons seek help in uncovering their stories for the negative contributions to their lives. I suspect this reticence, reluctance, and resistance in uncovering our stories derives from the divine illusion. If we have become Christians called by God, then our past has no power or control over our lives. Unfortunately, such thinking reeks of error. How much better is it to uncover our stories with all its strengths and vulnerabilities and allow God to bring strength and healing wherever needed!

How Family Influences Ministry

So far I have largely spoken about relational patterns and to a lesser extent on the drivenness apparent in his pursuit of ministry. I have focused on the personal implications, although at times I have moved into the areas where ministry was impacted. This is somewhat unavoidable because of how life and ministry intersect. However, in the rest of this chapter, I wish to focus more specifically on the impact of story in Wesley's life and the possible ministry implications. Specifically, I will discuss several issues including how one's story influences experience and response to the call; and how story can give direction and shape to one's ministry.

Family Background and the Call to Ministry

One way in which family might influence ministry relates to the area of call. Sometimes, we may think our call to ministry comes unadulterated, informed only by divine Word and validated by ecclesial confirmation. But calling comes to us in far more complex ways.[62] Sometimes call begins with someone sensing the gifts and characteristics consistent with a particular vocation within an individual, and alerting the person to this possibility. This was true in my own case. Long before I had any inkling God might be calling me to ministry, several persons alerted me to such a possibility (which I fervently resented). Over the years, I have heard similar stories from other persons in ministry. Sometimes the individual who did the alerting was a family member, and at other times, it was a leader or acquaintance in the church. However it happens, others often play a role in the way in which we experience call. Sometimes, the first inkling of call begins with our awareness of interests and preferences best suited to careers in ministry vocations. Sometimes, thoughts about a calling to a ministry vocation may present itself to us because everyone in our immediate environment engages in this profession. This becomes particularly compelling when the environment is our own family.

What does this line of discussion have to do with John Wesley and his experience of call? In chapter 5, I presented a genogram on the vocational themes within the Wesley family. In that genogram, it seemed impossible to miss the predominance of clergy on both the Annesley and Wesley sides of the family. Much like the Levitical priesthood, serving in holy orders was the family business. Males in the Wesley family naturally seemed to gravitate in this direction. The dominance of this career likely exerted an implicit pressure on males in the family to pursue the same path. Moreover, this preponderance might have contributed to a family belief, which dictated ministry as the most viable and logical option for males. Given this belief, influential males in the family would likely exert overt pressure on its male members to pursue this vocational direction. This was true both for Charles and John Wesley. John persuaded his brother Charles to enter Holy Orders against the latter's own wishes and his dread of taking such a step. John even persuaded him to accompany him and Oglethorpe on the mission to Georgia, again, against Charles' desire.[63] Years earlier, when he was twenty-two years old, John, himself, reported vocational pressure from his father to enter holy orders,[64] though this perspective has been disputed. Instead, Baker indicated the initiative

62. Guinness, *The Call*; Smith, *Listening to God*.
63. Lloyd, *Charles Wesley*.
64. Curnock, "The Journal"; Ward and Heitzenrater, *The Works*.

to enter ministry came from John, himself.[65] Perhaps the truth in this regard is far more complex, embracing Wesley's own statement as well as Baker's rebuttal. Wesley's call likely was influenced not only by his own initiative, but also reinforced by the urgings of his father and the powerful clerical line among his ancestors.

Acknowledging the contributions of family to one's calling into ministry does not necessarily negate the presence of a real, personal call from God. It merely affirms the complexity of calling as well as the significant influence family can exert on one's ministry direction. This same truth applies to other careers. Research has demonstrated how careers in one's family of origin consistently influences one's vocational aspirations.[66] In a class on career counseling, which I teach, I have discovered the same pattern. In it, I have consistently observed the strong influence of family career patterns on the vocational aspirations of class members. And though this influence proves powerful, students seem initially oblivious to its impact. Only in hindsight, and after they have drawn and analyzed their career genograms, do they seem to gain an awareness of how vocational dynamics in the family influenced them. But, in order to function well in ministry, one ought to become cognizant of the various forces, including family, which have influenced one's vocational direction. Such awareness can help one to sort out one's motivations and subsequent interests.

Wesley's Story and the Direction and Shape of his Ministry

Besides the likely influence of family dynamics in informing his call and response to it, Wesley's story also provided direction and shape to his ministry. Simply said, it shaped, to a great measure, the ways he functioned in ministry as well as dictated various emphases apparent within it. As indicated in earlier chapters, we see this shaping in several areas. We saw it in his emphasis on Scripture, education, missions, writing, publishing, and hymnody, as well as his love for the Anglican Church and its liturgy and sacraments. Each of these areas involved positive contributions gleaned from his family tree.[67] I shall not discuss these in any detail beyond that already covered in chapter 5. Instead, I shall discuss other dynamics evident in his narrative.

65. Baker, *Church of England*.
66. Brown and Brooks, *Career Counseling Techniques*.
67. Edwards, *Family Circle*; *Sons to Samuel*.

In an earlier chapter, I referred to John Wesley as the family star; that is, because of several converging circumstances surrounding his birth, he became a central figure in his family. One possible outgrowth of this role relates to the authority he seemed to exert over others. We saw this ability to exert authority and influence with his brother Charles, who deferred to him on many matters.[68] But John seemed to possess the uncanny ability to rule other persons, exacting deference, as well as the love of others.[69] Moreover, Wesley's central role in the family apparently made him one whom other family members sought out for attention, advice, and encouragement. His sisters especially sought him out for advice on a variety of issues, including problems in their intimate relationships. They also seemed to compete for his attention with each other. In a sense, Wesley became their counselor on varied matters important to them. In a letter written on August 13, 1735, his sister Emilia indicated she had especially chosen him from their childhood to serve as her companion and counselor in joy and griefs. Moreover, from her statement, it appears he alone among her family members served in this role.[70] This represents a profound acknowledgement, especially when one considers their difference in age. Emilia was his eldest living sister, some eleven years older than John. Thus, it seems fair to conclude John must have assumed this role in Emilia's life at a relatively young age.

Besides Emilia, his other sisters also wrote him about matters including their varied troubles, illnesses, and depression. In one letter to John on July 13, 1744, Hetty wrote describing herself as being "daily in heaviness thro many temptations."[71] The phrase caught my attention, since I knew it as the title of Wesley's sermon 47 "Heaviness through Manifold Temptations." This sermon is variously dated on May 5, 1754 or in 1760 depending on whether one follows Timothy L. Smith or Albert Outler respectively[72] Of course, the words for this sermon's title come directly from the text of I Peter 1:6. However, I could not help wondering if Hetty's letter, written years earlier, might have partly provoked this message. Given the many references to depression in the Wesley family letters, this

68. Lloyd, *Charles Wesley*.

69. Abelove, *Evangelist of Desire*.

70. Wesley, E., "Letter to John Wesley," August 13, 1735.

71. Wright, "Letter from Bristol," July 13, 1744.

72. Online, "The Sermons of John Wesley."

reality might also have contributed to such a sermon. After all, sermons not only find their inspiration in Scripture, sometimes circumstances and conditions which preachers encounter, also become motivation for the messages preached. Nevertheless, my main point in this discussion is to demonstrate how Wesley became a counselor to his sisters and reprised this role in conducting his broader ministry. Not surprisingly, he also reprised this role in his relationship to the many women to whom he wrote. In the many letters to women such as Sarah Ryan, Mary Bishop, and Ann Bolton, Wesley functioned in the role of spiritual counselor, a role that seemed apparent with his sisters. Moreover, like his sisters, these women, too, were drawn to him in affection and respect.[73] But, perhaps his relationship to his sisters and other family members also gave rise to other aspects of ministry, such as the sermons he preached.

That Wesley should reprise a family role in his ministry might seem surprising to some, but it ought not be. In fact, reenacting family roles within our current lives and work situations is all too common an occurrence.[74] This arises because such roles become ingrained in our nature and become a part of our habitual way of functioning. Reenacting family roles is not always a bad thing. Sometimes these roles carry implicit strengths within them and can contribute to the greater good. At other times, reenacting these roles can create complications in one's life and ministry. However, whether good or bad, reenacting family roles can unearth devastating consequences when the individual remains unaware of, and unconsciously functions out of, these roles. It is the unconscious reenacting of family roles that contributes to problems in over-functioning, self-sacrifice, or playing the hero.[75] Unfortunately, such roles sometimes exact a spiritual toll. Speaking about over-functioning, one author offered the following, "One of the subtlest, yet most fundamental, effects of over functioning is spiritual. It destroys the spiritual quality of the over functioner."[76]

Besides possible reenactment of roles played in the family, one can consider other factors, which might have shaped the direction and interests evident in John Wesley's ministry. In chapter 5, I discussed how Wesley's

73. Edwards, *Astonishing Youth*.

74. Friedman, *From Generation to Generation*; Steinke, *How Your Church Family Works*.

75. Friedman, *From Generation to Generation*; Wimberly, "Wife of 5 Years."

76. Friedman, *From Generation to Generation*, 212.

interest in treating physical and other ailments likely, and partly, developed from the presence of medical practitioners in his family tree. Furthermore, I suggested persistent and frequent illness in the family also contributed to this interest in health and wholeness. But, even when one moves beyond this arena, one yet finds linkages that seem to partly explain other interests fulfilled in his ministry. For example, Wesley placed great emphasis on the value of good stewardship in financial matters. His famous maxim, "Earn all you can, save all you can, give all you can," supports this emphasis on stewardship. One can rightly ground this principle about money on Scriptural grounds. In fact, we find this principle emphasized in his sermon titled "The Danger of Riches," based on I Timothy 6:9, and in a similar emphasis in his sermon on "Causes of the Inefficacy of Christianity," based on Jeremiah 8:22. But, might not this constant emphasis have also arisen from the pecuniary problems evident in his family? One might recall that the family struggled mightily with poverty, attributable to a large degree to the poor financial management skills of John's father, Samuel. It seems inconceivable that this deprived background would not have fostered some keen attention to financial matters.

My major point throughout this book has been to demonstrate, to some degree, how one's family can become a crucible giving shape to life and ministry. Specifically, I have tried to demonstrate this thesis in relation to the life of Methodism's founder, John Wesley. Admittedly, I cannot definitively prove all of the conclusions presented in this book. Hopefully, I have presented sufficient evidence and demonstrated enough linkages to lend some plausibility to the hypotheses presented here. In short, John Wesley appears a lot like we are. Even though redeemed by God and called to professional ministry, we all, including luminaries like John Wesley, remain undeniably human. As humans reared in homes with varied emotional climates and conditions, our families have inevitably deeply and powerfully shaped us, consciously and unconsciously. After all, the family remains a crucible for all of us, shaping us by the swirling forces engendered therein. Indeed, family remains for much of us the primary shaper through much of our lives. This truth remains, whether we minister in relative obscurity or whether we spawn a worldwide Christian movement as Wesley did. Because of the power of our family and the narratives it helps birth in us, understanding our story becomes of paramount importance. By so doing, we have the opportunity to glean from the assets and vulnerabilities evident therein. Furthermore, by understanding this story, we can make better sense of our varied beliefs, responses, and behaviors in life and ministry. Ultimately, success in life and ministry might well depend on how well we understand our family story, and how well we are able to navigate its rapids as we try to become the person and minister God created us to be.

Postscript

In the introduction to this document, I raised a possible issue relative to making inquiries into to Wesley's life; namely, such an endeavor could sully the reputation of this great Christian man. Given this way of thinking, writing this book about his life and ministry could possibly have reshaped my opinions about him. More specifically, uncovering a few vulnerabilities in his upbringing, which might have fashioned his life and ministry in some unfavorable ways, could lead one to hold a lesser opinion of him. This has not proven true in my case. I still confess myself an admirer of Wesley. However, I think I now possess a better grasp and understanding of Wesley's humanity. By peering more deeply into his human circumstances, I stand amazed at his ability to transcend, in some measure, his family of origin issues and to influence a nation and the world. Of course, one cannot simply attribute this to Wesley but to the grace of God working in him and his varied circumstances. Wesley stands as a shining example of what God can do in a life totally committed to him. Such lives still are encompassed by varied infirmities and vulnerabilities, but in the end, these cannot totally impede the grace and wonderful workings of God. Though I remain an admirer of Wesley, I confess, at times during the research and writing of this book, I have deeply grieved for Wesley as he wrestled with the all too human need and quest for love, intimacy, and companionship, only to be thwarted at every turn. Though we could legitimately lay some of this blame at his door, one should not forget the powerful legacies from his family of origin with which he struggled. In the end, family remained for Wesley as it does for all of us, a crucible.

Bibliography

Abelove, H. *Evangelist of Desire: John Wesley and the Methodists*. Stanford, CA: Stanford University Press, 1990.

Adler, A. *The Practice and Theory of Individual Psychology*. Rev. ed. London: Kegan Paul, Trench, Trubner and Co., 1929a.

———. *The Science of Living*. New York: Greenberg, 1929b.

———. *Significance of Earliest Recollections*. International Journal of Individual Psychology, 3, 283–87, 1937.

———. *The Individual Psychology of Alfred Adler: A Systematic Presentation in Selections from His Writings*. 1st ed. New York: Basic Books, 1956.

Annesley, A. Letter from Anne Annesley to Susanna Wesley, 12 August, 1731. (DDWF:4/1). Manchester, England: Methodist Church Archives, John Rylands University Library, 1731.

Baker, F. "Investigating Wesley Family Traditions." Methodist History. 26(3), 154–62, 1988.

———. John Wesley's First Marriage. Duke Divinity School Review, 31(3), 175–88, 1966.

———. *John Wesley and the Church of England*. London: Epworth Press, 1970.

———. Some Observations on John's Wesley's Relationship with Grace Murray. Methodist History, 16(1), 42–45, 1977.

Black, J. *A New History of England*. Gloucestershire: Sutton Publishing Limited, 2000.

Bleiberg, J. R., and Skufca, L. "Clergy Dual Relationships, Boundaries and Attachment." Pastoral Psychology. 54(1), 3–21, 2005.

Blessing, K. "Murray Bowen's Family Systems Theory as Bible Hermeneutic." Journal of Psychology and Christianity. 19(1), 38–46, 2000.

———. *Psychology and the Bible: A New Way to Read the Scriptures*. J. H. Ellen and W. G. Rollins (eds.), *From Gospels to Gnostics* (Vol. 3, 165–91). Westport, CT: Praeger Publishers/Greenwood Publishing Group, 2004.

Boss, Pauline. *Family Stress Mangement*. Newbury Park, CA: Sage Publications, 1988.

Bowen, M. "Toward the Differentiation of Self in One's Family of Origin." In F. Andres and J. Lorio (Eds.), Georgetown Family Symposia (Vol. 1). Washington, D. C.: Department of Psychiatry: Georgetown University Medical Center, 1974.

———. *Theory in the Practice of Psychotherapy*. In P. J. Guerin (Ed.), Family Therapy: Theory and Practice. New York: Gardner Press, 1976.

———. *Family Therapy in Clinical Practice*. New York: J. Aronson, 1978.

Brown, D., and Brooks, L. *Career Counseling Techniques*. Boston: Allyn and Bacon, 1991.

Brown, E. K. *Women in Mr. Wesley's Methodism*. Lewiston, New York: Edwin Mellon, 1983.

Carter, E. A., and McGoldrick, M. *The Family Life Cycle: A Framework for Family Therapy*. New York: Gardner Press, 1980.

————. *The Changing Family Lifecycle: A Framework for Family Therapy (2nd ed.)*. New York: Gardner Press, 1988.

Clarke, A. *Memoirs of the Wesley Family (Second ed.)*. New York: Lane and Tippett, 1846.

Coe, B. W. *John Wesley and Marriage*. Bethlehem London. Cranbury, NJ: Lehigh University Press; Associated University Presses, 1996.

Collins, K. J. "John Wesley's Relationship with his Wife as Revealed in his Correspondence." *Methodist History*. 32(1), 4–18, 1993.

————. *A Real Christian*. Nashville: Abingdon Press, 1999.

Corey, G. *Theory and Practice of Group Counseling (6 ed.)*. Belmont, CA: Brooks/Cole, 2004.

Corey, M. S., and Corey, G. *Becoming a Helper (5 ed.)*. Pacific Grove, CA: Brooks/Cole, 2006.

Curnock, N. "The Journal of the Rev. John Wesley, A.M." London: Charles H. Kelly, 1909.

Dallimore, A. A. *Susanna: The Mother of John and Charles Wesley*. Darlington Co., Durham: Evangelical Press, 1992.

Deepti. "Traces of the Past." Retrieved 2/3/08. http://www.tribuneindia.com/2001/2001 0519/windows/roots.htm.

Dobree, B. *Biography of John Wesley*. Albany, OR: Ages Software, 1997.

Dunton, J. *The Life and Errors of John Dunton*. New York: Burt Franklin, 1969.

Edwards, M. *My Dear Sister*. Manchester, England: Record (Offset) Ltd, 1974.

Edwards, M. L. *Family Circle: A Study of the Epworth Household in Relation to John and Charles Wesley*. London: Epworth Press, 1949.

————. *The Astonishing Youth: A Study of John Wesley as Men Saw Him*. London: Epworth Press, 1959.

————. *Sons to Samuel*. London: Epworth Press, 1961.

Egan, G. *The Skilled Helper (7 ed.)*. Pacific Grove, CA: Brooks/Cole Publishing Co., 2008.

English, J. C. "'Dear Sister': John Wesley and the Women of Early Methodism." *Methodist History*. 33(1), 26–33, 1994.

Ethridge, W. S. *Strange Fires: The True Story of John Wesley's Love Affair in Georgia*. Birmingham, Alabama: Vanguard, 1971.

Fowler, James. *John Wesley's Pilgrimage*. Wilmore, KY: Asbury Theological Seminary, 1991.

Friedman, E. *From Generation to Generation: Family Process in Church and Synagogue*. New York: Guilford Press, 1985.

Gilbert, C. "Catherine Gilbert to Charles Wesley." Unpublished Letter. Manchester, England: Methodist Church Archives, John Rylands University Library, 1740.

Green, V. H. H. *The Young Mr. Wesley: A Study of John Wesley and Oxfo*. New York: St. Martin's Press, 1961.

Grenz, S., and Bell, R. D. *Betrayal of Trust: Sexual Misconduct in the Pastorate*. Downers Grove, IL: Intervarsity Press, 1995.

Grolier Incorporated. *The New Book of Knowledge*, Vol. 5. 1982.

Guinness, O. *The Call: Finding and Fulfilling the Central Purpose of Your Life*. Waco, TX: Word, 1998.

Headley, A. J. "Anne Wesley: The Rest of the Story." Unpublished manuscript, Asbury Theological Seminary, 2008.

―――. *Created for Responsiility.* Anderson, IN: Bristol House Ltd, 2006.

Heitzenrater, R. P. *The Elusive Mr. Wesley.* Nashville: Abingdon Press, 1984.

―――. *Wesley and the People Called Methodists.* Nashville: Abingdon Press, 1995.

Hill, A. W. *John Wesley Among the Physicians.* London: The Epworth Press, 1958.

Jackson, T. (Ed.). "The Works of John Wesley," Third ed. Vol. 13. London: John Mason, 1829.

Kane, M. "Sexual Misconduct, Non Sexual Touch, and Dual Relationships: Risks for Priest in Light of the Code of Pastoral Conduct." Review of Religious Research. 48(1), 105–10, 2006.

Kimbrough, S. T., and Beckerlegge, O. A. (Eds.). "The Unpublished Poetry of Charles Wesley." Nashville, Tenn.: Kingswood Books, 1988.

Kirk, John. *The Mother of The Wesleys: A Biography.* Cincinnati: Jennings and Graham, 1865.

Kottler, J. *Good, Bad and Ugly Therapy.* Louisville, KY, 2005.

Lambert, A. "Letter to John Wesley at the New Room Bristol," January 12, 1741. (DDWF:10/1). Manchester, England: Methodist Church Archives: John Rylands University Library, 1741.

Lloyd, G. *Charles Wesley: A New Evaluation of his Life and Ministry.* Liverpool, 2002.

Maser, F. E. "John Wesley's Only Marriage: An Examination of Dr. Frank Baker's article 'John Wesley's First Marriage.'" Methodist History. 16(1), 33–41, 1977.

―――. *The Story of John Wesley's Sisters: Seven Sisters in Search of Love.* Rutland, VT: Academy Books, 1988.

McGoldrick, M., and Gerson, R. *Genograms in Family Assessment (First ed.).* New York: W.W. Norton and Company, 1985.

McGoldrick, M., Gerson, R., and Shellenberger, S. *Genograms: Assessment and Intervention.* New York: W. W. Norton and Company, 1999.

Moore, R. L. *John Wesley and Authority: A Psychological Perspective.* Missoula, Mont.: Scholars Press, 1979.

Mosak, H. H. "Adlerian Psychotherapy." In R. J. Corsini and D. Wedding (Eds.), Current Psychotherapies (Fourth ed.). Itasca, Illinois: F.E. Peacock Publishers, Inc., 1989.

Nichols, M. *Family Therapy: Concepts and Methods.* Needham Heights, MA: Allyn and Bacon, 1984.

Nichols, M. P., and Schwartz, R. C. *Family Therapy: Concepts and Methods.* Boston: Allyn and Bacon, 1998.

Online, W. C. "The Sermons of John Wesley 1872 Edition, Chronologically Ordered." Retrieved July 28, from Wesley Center for Applied Theology: Northwestern Nazarene University, 2009.

Pudney, J. *John Wesley and His World.* New York: Charles Scribner's Sons, 1978.

Rack, H. D. *Reasonable Enthusiast: John Wesley and the Rise of Methodism.* London: Epworth Press, 1989.

Reid, Marguerite. "Clinical Research: The inner world of the mother and her new baby—born in the shadow of death." Journal of Child Psychotherapy. Vol. 29, 2, 207–26, 2003.

Rogal, S. J. "John Wesley Takes a Wife." Methodist History. 27(1), 48–55, 1988.

―――. "Ladies Huntington, Glenorchy, and Maxwell: Militant Methodist Women." Methodist History. 32(2), 126–32, 1994.

————. *Susanna Annesley Wesley (1669–1742): A Biography of Strength and Love (The Mother of John and Charles Wesley).* Bristol, Ind.: Wyndham Hall Press, 2001.

Scanzoni, J. "Resolution of Occupational-Conjugal Role Conflict in Clergy Marriages." Journal of Marriage and Family, 27(3), 396–402, 1965.

Schwab, Reiko. "Parental Mourning and Children's Behavior." Journal of Counseling and Development, Vol. 57, 258–65, 1997.

Skowron, E. A. "The Role of Differentiation of Self in Marital Adjustment." Journal of Counseling Psychology. 47(2), 229–37, 2000.

Smith, G. *Listening to God in Times of Choice.* Downers Grove, IL: Intervarsity Press, 1997.

Southey, R. *The Life of John Wesley and the Rise and Progress of Methodism.* London: George Bell and Sons, 1890.

Steinke, P. *How Your Church Family Works: Understanding Congregations as Emotional Systems.* Washington, D.C.: Alban Institute, 1993.

————. *Healthy Congregations: A Systems Approach (2nd ed.).* Herndon, Va.: Alban Institute, 2006.

Stevenson, G. J. *Memorials of the Wesley Family.* London: S. W. Partridge and Co., 1876.

Telford, J. *The Letters of the Rev. John Wesley, A.M.* London: The Epworth Press, 1931.

————. *The Life of John Wesley.* New York: Phillips and Hunt, 1887.

Tipton, J. "Blessed Child Eases Pain of Tragedy: Second Kelenna Helps Heal Parents' Hearts." Lexington Herald Leader, November 16, 2003.

Titelman, P. "Emotional Cutoff in Bowen Family Systems Theory: An Overview. In P. Titelman (Ed.).

————, "Emotional Cutoff: Bowen Family Systems Theory Perspectives." New York: The Haworth Clinical Practice Press, 2003.

Tyerman, L. *The life and Times of the Rev. John Wesley, M.A., Founder the Methodists (2d ed.).* London: Hodder and Stoughton, 1872.

Valentine, S. R. *John Bennet and the Origins of Methodism and the Evangelical Revival in England.* Lanham, MD: Scarecrow Press, Inc., 1997.

Van Buren, A. "Wife of 5 Years Hasn't Moved in Yet." Lexington Herald Leader, February 6, 2009.

Walmsley, Robert. "John Wesley's Parents: Fire and Reconciliation." Manchester Guardian. July 3, 1953, p. 12, 1953.

Ward, R. W., and Heitzenrater, R. P. *The Works of John Wesley (Vol. 18).* Nashville: Abingdon Press, 1988.

Watts, M. R. *The Dissenters.* Oxford: Clarendon Press, 1978.

Wesley, C. *The Journal of the Rev. Charles Wesley, M.A. (Vol. 1).* Grand Rapids, Michigan: Baker Book House, 1980a.

————. *The Journal of the Rev. Charles Wesley, M.A. (Vol. 2).* Grand Rapids, Michigan: Baker Book House, 1980b.

Wesley, E. "Letter from Lincoln to John Wesley, December 31, 1729." (DDWF: 6/2). Manchester, England: Methodist Church Archives, John Rylands University Library, 1729.

————. "Letter to John Wesley, April 7, 1725." (DDWF:6/1). Manchester, England: Methodist Church Archives, John Rylands University Library, 1725.

————. "Letter to John Wesley, February 9, 1730." (DDWF:6/3). Manchester, England: Methodist Church Archives, John Rylands University Library, 1730a.

————. "Letter to John Wesley, March 14, 1730." (DDWF:6/4). Manchester, England: Methodist Church Archives, John Rylands University Library, 1730b.

————. "Letter to John Wesley, October 5, 1730." (DDWF:6/5). Manchester, England: Methodist Church Archives, John Rylands University Library, 1730c.

————. "Letter to John Wesley, February 7, 1734." (DDWF:6/7). Manchester, England: Methodist Church Archives, John Rylands University Library, 1734.

————. "Letter to John Wesley, August 13, 1735." (DDWF:6/8). Manchester, England: Methodist Church Archives, John Rylands University Library, 1735.

Wesley, K. "Letter to John Wesley, July 3, 1734." (DDWF 13/6A). Manchester, England: Methodist Church Archives, John Rylands University Library, 1734.

Wesley, Martha. "Letter to John Wesley at Lincoln College, June 22, 1734." (DDWF 12/5). Manchester, England: Methodist Church Archives, John Rylands University Library, 1734.

————. "Letter to John Wesley, February 7, 1727." (DDWF 12/2). Manchester, England: Methodist Church Archives, John Rylands University Library, 1727.

Wesley, Mary. "Letter to John Wesley at Lincoln College, Oxford, January 20, 1727." (DDWF 8/1). Manchester, England: Methodist Church Archives, John Rylands University Library, 1727.

Wesley, Samuel. "Letter to Archbishop John Sharpe of York, May 18, 1701." (DDWF 1/1). Manchester, England: Methodist Church Archives, John Rylands University Library, 1701.

————. "Letter from Wroot to John and Charles Wesley, 21 June 1727." (DDWF 1/7). Manchester, England: Methodist Church Archives, John Rylands University Library, 1727a.

————. "Letter from Wroot To John and Charles Wesley, 5 Jul 1727." (DDWF 1/8). Manchester, England: Methodist Church Archives, John Rylands University Library, 1727b.

————. "Letter from Epworth to John Wesley at Lincoln. 21 January, 1935." (DDWF1/12). Manchester, England: Methodist Church Archives, John Rylands University Library, 1735.

————. "Letter from Wroot to John Wesley at Lincoln College, July 18, 1727." (DDWF 1/9). Manchester, England: Methodist Church Archives, John Rylands University Library, 1727c.

Wesley, Susanna. "Letter from Epworth to her brother Samuel Annesley expressing a wish that they be reconciled after a long period of silence, Jan 20, 1721 (her birthday)." (DDWF 2/5). Manchester, England: Methodist Church Archives, John Rylands University Library, 1721.

————. "Letter from Epworth to Samuel Wesley Junior, October 11, 1709." (DDWF 2/2). Manchester, England: Methodist Church Archives, John Rylands University Library, 1709.

————. "Letter to John Wesley at Lincoln College, 21 Feb. 1732." (DDWF 2/9). Manchester, England: Methodist Church Archives, John Rylands University Library, 1732a.

————. "Letter to John Wesley at Lincoln College, Jan 1, 1734." (DDWF 2/11). Manchester, England: Methodist Church Archives, John Rylands University Library, 1734a.

————. "Letter to John Wesley, Saturday 30 March, 1734." (DDWF 2/12). Manchester, England: Methodist Church Archives, John Rylands University Library, 1734b.

————. "Photographic copy of a letter to JW at Lincoln College, 25 Oct, 1732." (DDWF 2/10). Manchester, England: Methodist Church Archives, John Rylands University Library, 1732b.

Wesley, S. J. "Letter from Salisbury, Wiltshire to John Wesley on Passage to GA, April 29, 1736." (DDWF 5/12). Manchester, England: Methodist Church Archives, John Rylands University Library, 1736.

———. "Letter to his father, 11 May 1719." (DDWF5/3). Manchester, England: Methodist Church Archives, John Rylands University Library, 1719a.

———. "Letter to John Wesley at Epworth, 6 January 1728." (DDWF 5/7). Manchester, England: Methodist Church Archives, John Rylands University Library, 1728.

———. "Letter to John Wesley at Lincoln College, 10 Dec. 1726." (DDWF 5/5). Manchester, England: Methodist Church Archives, John Rylands University Library, 1726.

———. "Letter to John Wesley, 16 April 1739." (DDWF 5/15). Manchester, England: Methodist Church Archives, John Rylands University Library, 1739.

———. "Letter to Samuel Wesley Sr. at Epworth 29 August 1719." (DDWF 5/4). Manchester, England: Methodist Church Archives, John Rylands University Library, 1719b.

———. "Letter to Susanna Wesley, 3 July 1731." (DDWF 5/8). Manchester, England: Methodist Church Archives, John Rylands University Library, 1731.

Wimberly, E. P. *Recalling Our Own Stories: Spiritual Renewal in Religious Caregivers.* San Francisco: Jossey-Bass Inc., 1997.

Wright, H. "Letter from Bristol to John Wesley, July 13, 1744." (DDWF 9/3). Manchester, England: Methodist Church Archives, John Rylands University Library, 1744.

Yeich, B. *Conversation on John Wesley and Conversion Narratives in Early Methodism.* Didsbury, England, 2008.